THE VOYNICH MANUSCRIPT

THE VOYNICH MANUSCRIPT

THE WORLD'S MOST MYSTERIOUS AND ESOTERIC CODEX

Foreword by Dr Stephen Skinner
Introduction by Dr Rafał T Prinke & Dr René Zandbergen

WATKINS
Sharing Wisdom Since 1893

THE VOYNICH MANUSCRIPT

First published in the UK and USA in 2017 by
Watkins, an imprint of Watkins Media Limited
Unit 11, Shepperton House,
89-93 Shepperton Road, London N1 3DF

enquiries@watkinspublishing.com

Publisher: Etan Ilfeld
Managing Editor: Fiona Robertson
Editor: James Hodgson
Managing Designer: Karen Smith
Production: Uzma Taj

A CIP record for this book is available from the British Library

ISBN: 978-1-78678-077-5

10 9 8 7 6 5 4 3

Typeset in Adobe Jenner Pro and Agenda
Colour reproduction by XY Digital
Printed in China

www.watkinspublishing.com

CONTENTS

Foreword

Dr Stephen Skinner

The Unsolved Enigma
of the Voynich Manuscript

Dr Rafał T Prinke & Dr René Zandbergen

What fascinates me most about the Voynich Manuscript, above and beyond the historical puzzle and above and beyond how interesting it would be to know what it actually says, is the idea of an unreadable book … We have cognizance of the world by ordering all the information we come upon in relation to information that we have already accumulated – through patterns. An unreadable book in a non-English script, with no dictionary attached, is very puzzling. We become like linguistic oysters, we secrete around it, we encyst it into our metaphysic. But we don't know what it says, which always carries with it the possibility that it says something that would unhinge our conceptions of things or that its real message is its unreadability. It points to the Otherness of the nature of information, and is what is called in structuralism a "limit text". Certainly the Voynich Manuscript is the limit text of Western occultism. It is truly an occult book – one that no one can read.

From The Archaic Revival *by*
TERENCE MCKENNA *(1946–2000),*
American ethnobotanist and mystic

FOREWORD

Dr Stephen Skinner

I first examined the mysterious Voynich Manuscript in August 1976, on a monochrome microfilm which had been rather erratically filmed for me. The present volume is a significant advance on that, being in full colour, and does the work much greater justice. Over the ensuing 40 years I have returned to the Voynich Manuscript on a number of occasions, but I have to confess that it gives up its secrets very grudgingly.

A little more is known about the origins of the Voynich Manuscript than about its contents. Scientific analysis of the inks and the parchment has dated the work to the first half of the 15th century, but its provenance since then has been rather sketchy. The current best guesses about its chain of ownership are incorporated in the following introduction by Dr Rafał Prinke and Dr René Zandbergen. These scholars have the distinct advantage of having access to languages and manuscript collections in Eastern Europe not normally available to English-reading scholars. This has enabled them to gather a wealth of evidence about the manuscript's history, in particular during the period immediately after it came into the possession of Rudolf II, Holy Roman Emperor and King of Bohemia (modern-day Czech Republic), possibly in the late 16th century.

In 2004, Dr Zandbergen established what is probably the most comprehensive website devoted to the Voynich Manuscript (www.voynich.nu). The late Dr Donald Laycock, an old friend and distinguished linguist from Canberra University, also supplied material to this study. Don was fascinated by cryptography and texts like the Voynich, as well as the Enochian documents that contained the angelic language transmitted by the Elizabethan scholars Edward Kelley and Dr John Dee. It was during my collaboration with Don on John Dee's diaries that I first encountered the Voynich Manuscript. We were assembling the *Complete Enochian Dictionary* from the text of the angelic "Calls" that Dee and Kelley received from spirits (which they had assumed were angels). In an effort to find a parallel language, Don suggested we look into the Voynich Manuscript. Long conversations in the

Red Lion pub near to the British Museum followed, but in the end it became clear that there was no connection between the two texts. Don planned to do more research on the manuscript before his premature death, and one of his friends, Jacques Guy, who was also involved in Voynich research, made some of Don's material available.

Although John Dee is often suggested as a former owner of the Voynich, and was said to have sold it to Emperor Rudolf, I cannot find any of his typical annotations or ladder-like ownership symbol anywhere in the work, and further research by Dr Prinke now makes it seem a rather unlikely conjecture. After passing through a number of hands, the manuscript was finally brought to general public attention in 1911 or 1912 by Wilfrid Voynich, a Polish collector and rare book dealer. Today it resides in the Beinecke Rare Book and Manuscript Library at Yale University.

There were a number of suggestions that the manuscript was a hoax, before the scientific dating of the materials with which it was created. As for the text itself, although the cryptography has never been cracked, the establishment of word and syllable groupings has demonstrated that it probably holds meaning rather than just being gibberish. It seems less than likely that someone in the 15th century would go to such a degree of trouble to produce a fake. Estimates of the time involved to assemble the information, draw and paint the illustrations and then write the text range from three months to several years of painstaking work. The care that went into its production suggests that it is much more likely to be the secret notebook of a practitioner of medical, herbal and astrological arts who did not wish casual readers to look through his work.

Later in the same century, Leonardo da Vinci (1452–1519) also used cryptography and mirror writing to disguise his investigations from the casually curious, or perhaps more to the point, from the Inquisition, which would have certainly found much to question in his work. The practice of drawing the illustration first and then writing the text later was common to both Leonardo and the Voynich Manuscript. As a result some researchers have suggested that Leonardo was its author, but this seems very unlikely given the half-century lapse between the manuscript dating and the start of Leonardo's adulthood.

As we can't read the text, we have to rely to a large degree on the clues embedded in the illustrations to understand the Voynich Manuscript. Fortunately, the artworks are often very detailed and occur on almost every folio. The most famous of the visual clues hints at the place of origin of the work. It is a small sketch of a castle which has the "swallow-tail" or Ghibelline fortifications peculiar to northern Italy (in the upper right circle of the "Rosettes" page, f.86r). As the Ghibelline family supported the Holy Roman Emperor rather than the Pope, they would have had trade connections with Germany, and this might explain some of the Germanic influences that have been spotted in the manuscript, such as the crossbow used by the archer in the Sagittarius illustration (f.73v).

Several of the folios may eventually turn out to be particularly significant. These include a potential contents page on folio 66, where the "alphabet" appears to have been used to mark chapter numbers down the left-hand column, much as both Hebrew and Greek use their alphabets to represent numbers.

The manuscript breaks down into the following clearly identifiable sections:

☀ a herbal or botanical section
☀ a cosmological section containing astronomical diagrams, organic-looking images of stars and recognizable zodiacal signs
☀ a section showing naked women bathing in elaborately reticulated baths
☀ a pharmaceutical section showing herb parts and traditional storage vessels
☀ a concluding block of solid textual material, often called the recipes section

These sections, as well as the history and interpretation of the manuscript, are described in more detail in Prinke and Zandbergen's introduction. The following gives an overview and presents some of my own theories regarding certain aspects of the Voynich Manuscript.

The work begins with an extensive botanical section running through folios 1–57, 65–66, 87, 90, 93–96 and again (but in a different style, showing plant parts rather than whole plants) in the pharmaceutical section in folios 88–89 and 99–102. Many of the plant illustrations focus on seeds, rhizomes and roots, which are the parts most often used in medicines. This supports the idea that the author was a physician or at least a herbalist. Many of the drawings are quite detailed, like the plant on folio 23r, which has an extended underground rhizome linking up separate plant stems. In theory, this should make the plants easy to identify, and then it should be possible to match the cryptographic label for each plant against Latin, Greek or Hebrew equivalents, helping to decipher the text as a whole. In practice, however, identification has been hampered by a number of difficulties, including the following:

☀ The plant name is never the first word on the page, or at least has not been found to be so.[1] In fact, a number of the lines begin with elaborate "gallows" symbols, which resemble standard Latin manuscript contractions for "pre", "pro" or "para" or may be read simply as meaningless flourishes.

☀ Some plant species may have become extinct over the passage of the last 600 years.

☀ Other plants may have changed due to changing methods of cultivation. A number of illustrations indicate advanced cultivation methods, such as grafting (folios 11r, 13r, 14r, 16r, 19v and 36r, for example).

☀ The labels may also include extra letters representing prepositions, conjunctions or definite or indefinite articles, which obscure the translation of the plant's name.

In recent years some researchers appear to have made progress in identifying some of the plants. One such researcher, Dr Edith Sherwood, has, to her own satisfaction, identified about 124 of a total of 126 botanical illustrations in the manuscript. Sherwood has also provided decodings of some of the plant names which she believes were written in reversed or mirror-letter Italian. Her work builds on that of Sergio Toresella, an expert in ancient herbals, who identified the script associated with the herbal drawings as consistent with documents from northern Italy written around the year 1460. Referring to John Florio's 1611 Italian dictionary,[2] Sherwood has proposed decoded versions of as many as 111 of the plant names, which would suggest that they were not only visually identifiable, but also all potentially labelled by the original scribe. This is a very recent advance which has led her to draw significant conclusions about letter equivalences to the script based on known plant identifications like sumac.

We can safely ignore Sherwood's penchant for identifying the work as that of Leonardo da Vinci, as this relies upon hidden and distorted supposed signatures, which are not very credible. However, her work on the Italian names of plants looks more solid now that she has been able to back them up with the Italian herbal labels. Nevertheless many identifications still seem speculative, but such research suggests that these plants were definitely drawn from real examples rather than being either the product of someone's overblown imagination, or the result of copying and re-copying dull medieval herbals. The vibrant detail and use of colour in these illustrations seemingly rules out the latter.

---

[1] German herbals from later in the 15th century often begin with the plant name, as do English herbals from the next century. This further suggests that the language is neither German nor English.

[2] *Queen Anna's New World of Words, or Dictionarie of the Italian and English Tongues*, by John Florio, 1598, expanded and reprinted 1611. The dedication was to Anne of Denmark, wife of James I of England.

Most of these plants were identified by Sherwood as growing around the Mediterranean littoral, with some (presumably brought home by explorers) from Asia and Africa. They would therefore have been known to Jewish, Greek or Italian physicians, but not necessarily in northern Europe. Many of the herbs appear in a 10th-century *Materia Medica* (based on Dioscorides), further strengthening the probability that the Voynich Manuscript was written by a physician. Many of the plants identified by Sherwood were thought in the 15th century to have medicinal properties, and many are still used in traditional remedies.

In the list below, using Sherwood's identifications[3], the name of the herb is followed by its Latin name, the manuscript folio number, its uses, the transliterated name in the text, and the plain text name of the herb in Italian (usually generated by reversing the order of the letters, or following some other anagrammatical method):

- French sage or mullein (incorrectly identified by Sherwood as *Salvia officianalis*) (f.3r), used in medicine and cookery (*cor vobas = vorbasco*)[4]
- Mallow (*Malva sylvestris*) (f.5v), used for coughs and sore throats (*olam = malo*)
- Violet (*Viola tricolor*) (f.9v), used in perfumery, has anti-viral properties (*voloi = violo* or *viola*)
- Turmeric (*Curcuma longa*) (f.11v), used as an antiviral and antibiotic, and in Indian cooking
- Black salsify or viper's grass (*Scorzonera*) (f.14r), used as a tonic and against snake bite
- Yam (*Dioscorea*) (f.17v), known to Portuguese explorers since the 14th century
- Greek valerian (*Polemonium caeruleum*) (f.19r), used for coughs and colds
- Woad (*Isatis tinctoria*) (f.25v), used as a blue dye in England and Tuscany
- Calendula, pot marigold (*Calendula officinalis*) (f.28v), used in ointments for burns, etc. (*alt ca = calta*)
- Wild marjoram (*Origanum vulgare*) (f.41r), used in poultices
- Lavender (*Lavandula angustifolia*) (f.45v), once used to ward off fleas and hence plague
- Lungwort (*Pulmonaria officinalis*) (f.47v), used for lung infections (*coiban = bianco*)

---

[3] www.edithsherwood.com/voynich-botanical-plant-anagrams/index.php?page=1

[4] *Vorbasco* or *Verbasco* is the Italian name for French sage or mullein. In this and the following examples, the last word in bracketed italics is the Italian word for each herb as found in Florio's dictionary. Where this does not appear, the identification comes from Sherwood's earlier work based solely on visual identification.

✳ Masterwort (*Astrantia major*) (f.50r), used for diseases of the stomach

✳ Cabbage thistle (*Cirsium oleraceum*) (f.54r), used in medicine and cookery
(*elcai oam = omacilea*)

✳ Harebell (*Campanula rotundifolia*) (f.32v) is a particularly convincing
visual identification

Other herbal drugs that would have been an important part of the physician's knowledge include cannabis (f.16r), whose properties are well enough known. The heads of the plant shown on folio 24 look very similar to the seed head of the opium poppy,[5] a plant long known to have medicinal value. It was introduced into Israel in ancient times and hence would have been available in Europe by the 15th century.

The second and third sections focus on cosmology, astronomy and astrology, but there are a few illustrations where plant life and astrology intermix. Specialized charts such as folio 67r2 show 12 phases of the moon (as distinct from 28 phases). Recognizable zodiacal and planetary sign illustrations include both the sun and the moon (f.67v1, f.68r1). Each zodiacal illustration has 30 naked women, each of whom is holding a star. These are likely to represent the 30 degrees of each sign (30 × 12 = 360 degrees of the zodiac).

No part of the Voynich Manuscript has baffled scholars more than the section featuring repeated drawings of naked women bathing in intestine-like bath systems (ff.75–84v). I think I can offer a possible explanation of these illustrations. The scenes resemble in concept, if not in actual structure, the communal baths known as *mikvoth* which were built by medieval Jews. Women were required to bathe in a *mikvah* to restore their ritual purity after menstruation or childbirth (or coming in contact with a dead body). This practice is still adhered to by Orthodox Jews. Another indication that the images depict a *mikvah*, rather than just a scene of casual bathing, is that the women are all completely naked with their sexual organs clearly visible. The *mikvah* was one of the few structures where women would wash together completely naked.

If the illustrations were depicting, for example, a Turkish or Roman bath, then the bathers would more likely be male or a mixture of sexes. If, as has sometimes been suggested, the illustrations symbolize intestines, then there is no conceivable reason why they would be populated by women.

---

[5] Sherwood very strangely identified this plant as a cucumber.

The amount of thought that went into the construction of *mikvoth* was considerable. They were carefully designed to drain away the polluted water without it being returned to the pure reservoir, and to replace it frequently with ritually pure water. As shown on folio 82 the author was quite concerned with the problems of water reticulation. If my conclusion is correct then undoubtedly the author and the cultural context of this manuscript are Jewish.

From Sherwood's research into the plant names, it is fairly certain that the manuscript is written in a combination of Latin and Italian concealed by two cryptographic tricks: reverse ordering and mirror writing of individual characters. There seem to be 17 characters, which can be seen most clearly on folio 57v, where they appear four times in the same sequence in the second ring. This sequence is partially repeated in the fourth circle. The first and third circles appear to contain separate words. The beginning of this sequence is marked by a word in the top left outside of the circles. It appears that a number of the symbols at the beginning of lines are meaningless flourishes, and should be ignored.

Continuous text appears at the end of the manuscript between folios 103 and 116. It contains 324 points marked by stars (some dark and some light). But two folios are missing. Speculatively, if those missing folios contained another 41 passages, then there would have been a total of 365 such passages. If this is the case then these passages might refer to the days of the year, with bright stars indicating good days and dark stars indicating bad days, or possibly best/worst days for treatment or surgery. Without the missing folios this theory is impossible to verify.

Although much about the Voynich Manuscript remains a mystery, I feel able to draw the following conclusions. It was probably the working handbook of an herbalist-astrologer-physician living in northern Italy (because of the Ghibelline castle architecture). If I am right about the *mikvah* illustrations then the author was almost certainly Jewish, and therefore the place of composition may have been a Jewish community in a northern Italian city such as Pisa. The Jewish hypothesis is also supported by the complete absence of any Christian imagery, unusual for the period.

Whatever the truth about this enigmatic work, the Voynich Manuscript will continue to fascinate and challenge readers for years to come. Eventually it will be cracked, because I am sure that it is not simply gibberish. When it is deciphered, I think we will find a significant text which will provide valuable information on astrological, medical and herbal learning of the early 15th century.

THE UNSOLVED ENIGMA OF THE VOYNICH MANUSCRIPT

by Dr Rafał T Prinke & Dr René Zandbergen

The Voynich Manuscript is a unique medieval manuscript, the only book in existence that has been written in this particular language and alphabet – a language that nobody can read. The manuscript is profusely illustrated, and these illustrations are also unique. In the following, we will briefly describe the manuscript: the materials it has been made of, the writing and the illustrations. We will discuss the known part of its history and the many attempts that have been made to translate it, and we will examine some of the most interesting statistical analyses of the text. Our approach is objective and critical, so we present only what is relatively certain about the contents and history of the Voynich Manuscript, and we highlight the problems associated with various unsupported claims to have "solved" the manuscript. In this way we hope to provide a foundation for further research and hypothesis.

Description of the manuscript

The Voynich Manuscript is a fairly small parchment codex. Comparable in size to a modern paperback, it measures about 23 × 16cm (9 × 6½in) and is about 5cm (2in) thick. It was written on parchment made of calf skin (as determined by a 2014 University of York study). This is of moderate quality; some folios have been cut from the edges of the skins, and some have small holes and tears. The material has, however, been prepared with great care, judging by its evenly pale colour on both sides; the hair and flesh sides are almost indistinguishable from each other. The first and last few folios have a number of small holes made by insects.

The cover of the codex is of blank parchment, with no indication of an author or a title. This cover was added by the Jesuits in Rome in the 19th century, replacing wooden boards probably covered by leather, which may be inferred from the insect holes on the first and last folios. The present limp cover was originally stiffened by filling material, but this has been removed, almost certainly by its then owner Wilfrid Voynich, in search of hidden treasures. This habit of Voynich has been documented by Helen Zimmern, who met him in his Florence book shop (Zimmern 1908).

The manuscript originally consisted of 116 numbered folios, but 14 of these are now lost. Yet another unusual aspect of the work is that a number of the folios fold out. Some are two or three times as wide as a normal folio, and fold to fit in the book. All folios are numbered in the upper right-hand corner in a hand that cannot be accurately dated; estimates range from the 15th to the 17th century. The folios were originally grouped into 20 quires, but two of these (16 and 18) are now lost. The quires have also been numbered, in what looks like an earlier hand than that used to number the folios. Although the quire and folio numbering proceeds consistently, there are various indications that the present order of the pages is not the same as originally intended by the author, which would suggest that the pages got out of order before the book was bound.

Almost all pages contain both drawings and text. We can be fairly certain that the author started by drafting the outlines of the illustrations first and then added the text, carefully avoiding the drawings. Finally, he would have painted within the outline drawings, often not very carefully, in several shades of green and brown, a dark blue and a light blue, red and a faded yellow. Thanks to chemical analysis by the McCrone Research Institute in Chicago, we know that the text and drawing outlines were rendered in an iron gall ink of a kind that was in use throughout most of the Middle Ages (Barabe 2009). The researchers also analyzed the pigments used for the painting, and found them to have been made mostly from relatively inexpensive ground minerals. The faded yellow colour was most probably an organic paint (Clarke 2011, Quandt 2015).

The text of the manuscript uses a unique alphabet, probably invented specifically for it. Some characters resemble normal Latin characters like a, o and c, while others look like numerals (4, 8, 9). The remaining characters are more unusual, but do have similarities with symbols used in abbreviations in medieval manuscripts. The number of individual characters cannot be counted exactly, since there appear to be some ligatures, but the total is usually estimated to be between 24 and 30. This estimate supports the theory that the script is alphabetic.

The text is generally written from left to right and from top to bottom, usually with a straight left margin, and all pages use the same set of characters. Paragraphs are clearly marked and individual words are separated by spaces. Some words occur often and others more rarely. Certain words appear throughout the manuscript. In fact, everything suggests that this is a completely normal text in a language that should be easy to figure out. In certain parts of the manuscript the text has been arranged to fit the illustrations. There are many circular diagrams, and the text is occasionally written around their circumferences or along their radii. One also finds individual words near drawings, which appear to be labels.

The sections of the manuscript

The Voynich Manuscript starts with a long herbal or botanical section, so called because it has large illustrations of herbs or plants, usually filling most of the page. This section occupies half of the pages in the manuscript. There are usually two or three paragraphs of text set apart from the drawings. Almost all of the botanical pages are devoted to a single herb, although in a few cases there are two. The nature of these illustrations has been the source of much debate. While there are many other herbal manuscripts from roughly the same era, their illustrations tend to be copied from one manuscript to the next, with some variations. However, the botanical drawings in the Voynich Manuscript do not match any of the other herbals. Some of them look realistic, while others appear to be imaginary plants, or composites showing leaves from one plant and flowers from another. Many researchers have tried to identify the plants in the manuscript, but as long as the text cannot be read, most of these identifications are tentative at best.

After the herbal section, there is a number of pages that can be subdivided into three related categories, namely astronomical, astrological and cosmological. Almost all of the drawings in this section are circular. Astronomical pages often have a sun or moon face in the centre or show arrangements of stars, and many of the stars have single-word labels next to them, possibly the names of the stars. The astrological pages have clearly recognizable depictions of the zodiac cycle, although not in the order one would expect. This zodiac starts with Pisces instead of Aries, the signs of Aries and Taurus are represented twice, and the cycle ends with Sagittarius. Capricorn and Aquarius are missing, but there is also a missing page in the manuscript where they should appear, so it is reasonable to assume that they were once there. The most conspicuous feature of the zodiac illustrations is that each of the zodiac emblems is surrounded by 30 small, mostly nude female figures, each holding a star. The double Aries and Taurus drawings have only 15 figures each, so the total is again 30. It seems most likely that these relate to the degrees of the zodiac. In addition, each figure with a star has a label.

Cosmological pages feature geometric designs which cannot easily be classified. The use of the term "cosmological" for these pages was introduced by the early researcher William Newbold (Newbold 1928). While some of these designs appear unique, others are quite similar to cosmological illustrations found in other medieval manuscripts, which relate to the months of the year, the zodiac or the winds. There is one very large composite drawing on a sextuple foldout page consisting of nine connecting circles with four smaller items in the corners. This is usually called the "Rosettes" page. It includes innumerable details, including several illustrations of buildings, one reminiscent of a northern Italian castle (already mentioned in the Foreword by Stephen Skinner). The central circle includes six tower-like structures supporting a plane filled with stars, which could represent the sky. Many people have considered that this drawing may represent a map, but this is not certain.

The following section of the codex has traditionally been called the biological section, though others prefer to call it the balneological section. Perhaps the most unusual part of the Voynich Manuscript, it contains drawings of the same type of female figures that feature in the zodiac section, but here they are populating arrangements of pipes or vessels, and what seem like baths or clouds. Many illustrations give the impression of representing a chemical (alchemical) or natural process. They have also been likened to organs in the human body. Most of the water in this section has been painted green, while smaller parts are blue. Several researchers have, independently, pointed out a similarity to the illustrations in the manuscripts of *De Balneis Puteolanis*, a description of medicinal baths written in the 13th century, which is why this section is often referred to as "balneological". The pages are filled with text from top to bottom, as always carefully avoiding the drawings, and most of the female figures are labelled.

The next part is usually called the pharmaceutical section. It consists of three double folios that are not bound together in the codex (one of the most compelling reasons to believe that the pages are not in the original order). Each of these has one foldout folio, and all pharmaceutical folios have a similar layout. On the left side of each page are objects that look like containers. Arranged to the right of these containers are arrays of small herbal drawings. Most of these are not complete herbs, but only leaves or roots. They differ in size, and almost all are accompanied by a label. This section is not similar to any other herbal manuscript. In a number of cases, the herb drawings in the pharmaceutical section are clearly copies of parts of other herbal drawings found elsewhere in the manuscript.

The containers appear in two main forms. They are either composed of two or three cylindrical sections getting narrower toward the top, or have a more complicated shape. Some of them appear empty, others appear to contain some liquid which has been painted in various colours. Some have a lid, some have feet. A few of the simple containers have also been compared to early microscopes, but this is problematic since such microscopes postdate the manuscript by more than 150 years.

At the end of the manuscript we find 12 unillustrated folios with text in many short paragraphs. This is usually called the recipes section. In the left margin of these pages are drawings of stars that usually (but not always) mark the start of a paragraph. These stars are similar in style to those in the zodiac section. They come in different types: the number of points is usually seven or eight. Some are painted red, and some have a red or faded yellow centre. Some have a dot in ink in the centre. On all folios except 103 and 116 the stars have tails. One other folio much earlier in the manuscript (f.58 in quire 8) has a similar lack of other illustrations, and a few stars in the margin on both the recto and verso side.

While essentially all of the text in the Voynich Manuscript has been written in its unique script, there are a number of annotations, possibly contemporary, but possibly also later, that include more or less legible text in the normal Latin alphabet. The best-known example is found on the verso of the last folio (f.116v). It consists of only four lines, and has a mixture of pseudo-Latin text, German words and two words in the Voynich script. There are crosses between many words, strongly suggesting that it is some kind of prayer or spell. Although there have been some proposed readings, even this supposedly legible part of the manuscript remains something of a mystery.

Certainly legible are the names of the months that a later owner of the manuscript has written near each of the zodiac emblems. These have been written in French, most probably a northern dialect. Whether the Voynich Manuscript was ever in northern France, and who might have owned it then, are further mysteries.

The history of the manuscript

Recent forensic investigations and new findings within the body of the Voynich Manuscript leave little doubt that it is of Germanic (Austrian or northern Italian) origin and was written in the first half of the 15th century. A radio-carbon dating analysis made in 2009 at the University of Arizona for an Austrian documentary by Andreas Sulzer and Klaus Steindl has dated the parchment to 1405–38 with 95 per cent probability (Hodgins 2012, Zandbergen 2012). This supports a proposal made by the iconologist Erwin Panofsky (1892–1968) in 1931 that the manuscript was certainly a mid-15th-century artefact on the basis of the style of its illustrations. Nothing else is known about the whereabouts of the manuscript until some two centuries later when it appeared in Prague, and since then its history is relatively well documented.

The Horčický-Sinapius signature

One of the key pieces of evidence enabling us to trace the ownership of the manuscript is a faint signature, now hardly visible, at the bottom of the first folio. At some time in the 1910s, Wilfrid Voynich enhanced it with chemicals and photographed it (Voynich 1921), while more recently it was examined under ultraviolet light for the 2009 Sulzer and Steindl documentary. The signature was found to read "Jacobj à Tepenecz No. [19?]", thus confirming Voynich's discovery that the manuscript once belonged to Jakub Horčický (1575–1622), also known under the latinized form of his name as Sinapius, to which the predicate "of Tepenec" was added after he was ennobled by Emperor Rudolf II in 1608. René Zandbergen located several other books from Horčický-Sinapius' library, all signed and numbered, some also dated. The earlier ones were signed as Sinapius, while those obtained after his ennoblement bear the same form of signature as that found in the Voynich Manuscript. He also numbered them separately and it seems that the number on the mysterious book is 19, but the reading is far from certain. In any case, he would have incorporated it into his library in 1608 or shortly afterwards (Prinke 2012).

Horčický-Sinapius was brought up by Jesuits who taught him herbal pharmacy. Educated at the Jesuit university Clementinum in Prague, he became the administrator of the Benedictine nunnery of St George in Prague Castle and sold his herbal medicines ("*aquae Sinapianae*") at the gate of the Jesuit garden located at the foot of the castle hill. In 1615 the rich Mělník estate was leased to him by Emperor Matthias and although he was arrested in 1618 by Protestant rebels and then exiled, he returned soon after their defeat in 1620 and continued to prosper. Two years later he died after falling off a horse and left an enormous sum of money to support poor students at the St Wenceslaus seminary (Schmidl 1754, Pelzel 1773–82, Smolka and Purš 2014).

From Rudolf II to Athanasius Kircher: *circa* 1600–1680

Perhaps the most important early source of information about the Voynich Manuscript is a letter written from Prague by Johannes Marcus Marci (Jan Marek Marci of Kronland, 1595–1667) to his friend Athanasius Kircher (1602–80) on 19 August 1665, in which he explained that he had inherited the book from another friend and was now sending it to Kircher because nobody else would be able to read it. Marci was 70 years old at the time and would die two years later. The letter was inserted into the book and preserved with it, so there should be no doubt it refers to the Voynich Manuscript rather than to some other work (Voynich 1921).

Both Marci and Kircher are well known as important early modern scholars and scientists. The former was a professor of medicine at Charles University (Carolinum) in Prague, the head physician of the kingdom of Bohemia and personal physician to two Holy Roman Emperors. In 1667 Marci was granted fellowship of the Royal Society of London in recognition of his scientific investigations. The most important of Marci's discoveries relate to the refraction of light and theory of colours, usually attributed to Isaac Newton, whom he preceded by at least 20 years (Svobodný 1998, Garber 2002). He had friendly relations with Jesuit scholars (traditional rivals of universities) and corresponded with some of them, including Athanasius Kircher, who was generally regarded by his contemporaries as the most learned polymath of his age.

Kircher published over 40 books, mostly large and lavishly illustrated volumes, on such diverse subjects as mathematics, physiology, magnetism, optics, linguistics, geology, biblical interpretation, history, archaeology, and others. Owing to his voluminous works on Egypt and China, Kircher is often called the founding father of modern Egyptology and sinology, while his ambitious (though largely mistaken) attempts to decipher Egyptian hieroglyphics earned him the fame of a great linguist among his contemporaries (Godwin 2009, Fletcher 2011). This reputation is also clear from Marci's letter, who wrote to Kircher that the Voynich Manuscript "can be read by none if not by you" and that "such riddles only obey their own Kircher" who can "break through [their] bars with your habitual ease" (Neal 2000–2010).

Kircher gathered much of the material for his books through an extensive network of correspondents, including not only Jesuits from all parts of the world, but also Protestant intellectuals (Fletcher 1988). Fortunately, over 2,000 of his letters survive and reside in the Historical Archives of the Pontifical Gregorian University in Rome. Earlier research by the renowned Kircher scholar John Fletcher had already shown that there were other letters from Marci, and also a much earlier one from a certain Georgius Barschius, dated 27 April 1639 (Fletcher 1972). Having seen Barschius mentioned as a lifelong friend in Marci's book *Philosophia Vetus Restituta* (1662), Voynich already suspected him as a previous owner of the manuscript, a suspicion that René Zandbergen confirmed by examining Barschius' letter. Most importantly, the letter corroborated the information from Marci's 1665 letter. It is also the earliest external source that clearly describes the same manuscript. Jorge Stolfi and Philip Neal later discovered and translated some more letters (by Marci and others) mentioning the Voynich Manuscript, allowing a reconstruction of the sequence of events.

In his 1639 letter, Barschius refers to an even earlier letter of 1637, which he sent to Kircher via the famous Jesuit mathematician Théodore Moret (Moretus, 1602–67) together with copies of some pages from the manuscript, and to which he had received no reply. He explained to Kircher that he was prompted to write by Kircher's publication of a dictionary of the Coptic language (1636) – he believed the manuscript contained secrets of Egyptian herbal medicine and chemistry, which only Kircher could unravel for the good of humanity.

Although Kircher did not reply directly to Barschius' 1637 letter, he did make a brief, enigmatic reference to "unintelligible writing" in a letter to Moretus from March 1639 that has recently been discovered by Josef Smolka. Given that this letter predated Barschius' 1639 letter by only a month, one may assume that Kircher was referring to the copied pages of the Voynich Manuscript and that this comment is what prompted Barschius to make a second attempt to contact Kircher (Smolka and Zandbergen 2010). However, it appears that Kircher still did not reply to Barschius, as two years later Marci, in his first known correspondence on the subject, reminded Kircher about the same undeciphered codex and sent him another copied page from "*amicus meus* M[agister] Georgius Barschius", describing his friend as "a man of the highest quality and greatly skilled in chemical matters". But Kircher apparently remained silent throughout, not responding even after Marci sent him the entire original manuscript 24 years later, in 1665. In 1666 a mutual friend of Marci and Kircher, Gottfried Aloys Kinner, asked Kircher about "the interpretation of that arcane book which he [Marci] gave up to you". He tried again in 1667, when Marci had "now fallen into the second infancy of old age", using the argument that "it will be a great solace to him if you are able to satisfy his curiosity on this point" (Neal 2000–2010).

Until recently, the identity of Barschius remained unknown. Besides references to him in the letters, he was mentioned by Marci in *Philosophia vetus restituta* as his lifelong friend, whom he had met 40 years earlier (i.e. in about 1622). He was "a man of great experience in chemical matters" and, as Marci related, "when he was dying he made me the inheritor of his collections and chemical library" – which confirms the statement from Marci's 1665 letter to Kircher. It is important that Marci stresses that Barschius never married, which excludes the possibility that he was a member of the clergy or a university professor. Catholic clergy and university professors were forbidden to get married, so if Barschius had been a member of one of these professions Marci would not have mentioned his unmarried state because it would have been obvious. However, Marci calls Barschius "magister", so he must have been a university graduate. This has been confirmed by Josef Smolka, who found out that "Georgius Barschius, Syncoviensis [i.e. from the town of Synkov]" studied at the Clementinum, receiving his baccalaureate in 1602, followed by a magisterium in 1603 (Smolka and Zandbergen 2010). From his own letter to Kircher it is also known that in 1605 he studied at La Sapienza in Rome (Fletcher 1972). Further research by Rafał T. Prinke showed that M[agister] Jiří Bareš received the citizenship of Prague Old Town in 1624 and presented the required letter of honest origin from the town of Častolovice near Synkov (Líva 1937). The name is obviously the Czech original of the latinized form used by Marci.

Significantly, Bareš-Barschius was at the Clementinum at the same time as Horčický-Sinapius. Moreover, like Horčický, he worked at the Royal Castle, specifically at the Highest Prague Burgrave Court of Justice, first as a scribe and then from 1630 until at least 1646 as a relator, a very high office in the legal hierarchy (Teige 1893, Vacek 1923). Having shared a place of study and work and an interest in alchemy and pharmacy, Bareš and Horčický would have known each other well. It is therefore quite likely that Horčický left the Voynich Manuscript to Bareš, who in turn bequeathed it to Marci, who sent it to Kircher in Rome. Kinner's 1667 letter to Kircher specifies that the codex was sent through the "Father Provincial" of the Bohemian Jesuits. The office was held at that time by Daniel Krupsky (1620–72), later also rector of the Clementinum. The question remains how and when Horčický became its owner.

In his 1665 letter, Marci informed Kircher that "Doctor Raphael, the Czech language tutor of King Ferdinand III [...], once told me that the said book belonged to Emperor Rudolf and that he presented 600 ducats to the messenger who brought him the book." Then he added that the same "Raphael thought that the author was Roger Bacon the Englishman" but "I suspend my judgement on the matter." The attribution to Bacon was clearly just a guess, perhaps to make Kircher more interested in the manuscript. Roger Bacon (1214–92) was at that time highly regarded in central Europe as a natural philosopher, inventor, alchemist and magician, and a number of his genuine and pseudepigraphic works were published there at the turn of the 17th century, both in Latin and in German translations. While that hypothesis of Marci's friend was clearly unfounded, he may have had reliable information about Rudolf II's ownership of the manuscript.

"Doctor Raphael" was Rafael Soběhrd Mnišovský of Sebuzín (1580–1644), a lawyer educated in Paris and Rome and an imperial counsellor, ennobled in 1621. He held numerous offices at the Court of Appeal, Court Chancellery, Royal Chamber, Lower Land Court and elsewhere, so he would certainly have had close contact with his contemporary Jiří Bareš of the Burgrave Court. He shared with Bareš a great interest in alchemy, as shown by his 1630 letter to Emperor Ferdinand II concerning his contacts with the Polish alchemist Michael Sendivogius (Podlaha 1903, Evans 1984). Holding such a privileged position, Mnišovský may have received the information about the manuscript from someone who had been close to Rudolf II and witnessed his purchasing it. The Emperor was famous for his extensive collections of art, books and curiosities. The sum he paid seems very high (600 ducats amounts to 2.1kg of gold, which would equate to approximately US$90,000 at the current price of gold) but René Zandbergen's analysis of the extant records of his expenditures shows that Rudolf paid even more for other books (Zandbergen and Prinke 2005, 2011).

It may, therefore, be accepted (with some caution) that an unidentified "messenger" brought the Voynich Manuscript to Prague, possibly at the end of the 16th century, and sold it to Rudolf, maybe even stating that it had been written by Roger Bacon, which would certainly justify the high price to anyone interested in alchemical secrets. As a reward for curing the Emperor of some illness at the end of winter 1608, Horčický was employed as a courtier and ennobled in the same year. Recognizing his expertise in herbal pharmacy, Rudolf may have also presented the curious codex to him at about that time, which Horčický signed and incorporated into his collection.

Concerning the mysterious "messenger" and previous owner of the Voynich Manuscript, it was suggested by Wilfrid Voynich himself that this may have been the English scholar Dr John Dee, who was interested in Roger Bacon and collected manuscripts from English monasteries abandoned after the Reformation (Voynich 1921). Some researchers have even identified the pagination of the codex folios as being in Dee's hand and have found a reference in the English doctor's diary to 630 ducats (Roberts and Watson 1990). On closer inspection, however, neither of these findings proved relevant, as the pagination digits were formed in a different way from those in Dee's genuine writings, while the money was in no way related to any book and in fact Dee received more than 2,000 ducats (Skinner 2012). All such speculations (including a possible role for Dee's companion Edward Kelley) may be safely discarded in view of the now well-established date and provenance of the Voynich Manuscript and the lack of any other indications that its origin might have been English. The most probable (but far from incontrovertible) scenario is that after the author's death the codex found its way into a monastery library in northern Italy or the southern borders of the Holy Roman Empire, where it was picked up by one of Rudolf's emissaries, who were always looking for curiosities for his collection.

From Kircher to Voynich: 1680–1912

Athanasius Kircher does not seem to have been greatly interested in the Voynich Manuscript. When he died in 1680, his library and archives were housed in the Jesuit Collegium Romanum, but other collections perished. Although early catalogues and descriptions of the original Musaeum Kircherianum (De Sepi 1678, Buonanni 1709) do not mention anything resembling the manuscript he had received from Marci, and some of his books and manuscripts were apparently moved around and divided among different collections, there is evidence to suggest that the Voynich Manuscript did end up in the Collegium. For example, many items in the Collegium Romanum library were rebound between 1824 and 1870, which matches the estimated date of the manuscript's present cover.

In 1873 the Italian government suppressed the Society of Jesus, confiscated all its possessions and converted the Collegium Romanum library into the National Library, to be enriched with collections from other monasteries. To save at least part of the original collection, slips of paper with the name of the Jesuit general, Pierre-Jean Beckx (1795–1887), were attached to as many of the Collegium Romanum books and manuscripts as possible, so that the works would be treated as his private library and not confiscated.

The exact route of the Voynich Manuscript at that time is still unclear. Most probably it was part of the collection of humanist and classical manuscripts which was moved outside Rome (quite possibly to the Villa Torlonia in Castel Gandolfo) in about 1873. Then sometime after 1903 – when the revived Society of Jesus decided to sell the collection to the Vatican – the manuscript found itself in the Villa Mondragone near Frascati, where it was purchased together with some other items by the antiquarian book dealer Wilfrid Voynich in 1911 or 1912. Having conducted the transaction in secrecy under the mediation of Joseph Strickland, an English Jesuit from Malta (1864–1917), Voynich always remained evasive about how he came to own the manuscript. He provided several accounts, one of which referred to a "castle in Austria". He also removed Beckx's ownership slips from all the books he had purchased from the collection. Still more perplexing is the uncorroborated claim by John Fletcher that after Kircher's death the Voynich Manuscript "was quietly passed on to some Farnese nobleman of the Court of Parma, and as quietly forgotten, until its rediscovery in 1912 [Fletcher gives this date as 1921, but this is clearly a typo]" (Fletcher 2011). Whichever (if any) of those versions is true, there is no doubt that the codex was purchased by Voynich and in 1912 he showed it to some scholars in France and England. He was so fascinated by the manuscript that he never sold it, and he never gave up trying to solve its mystery.

From Voynich to the Beinecke Library: 1912–present

The life of Wilfrid Michael Voynich (or Michał Wilfrid Habdank-Wojnicz) is as fascinating as the mysterious book that now bears his name. He was born on 31 October 1865 as a son of Leonard Wojnicz, a civil servant in the town of Telšė in Samogitia (now in Lithuania, at that time part of the Russian Empire). The family belonged to the lesser Polish nobility. Wilfrid studied pharmacy at Moscow University, where he became involved in anarchist revolutionary activities. Having moved to Warsaw he continued to work with the anarchists, which led to his arrest in 1885. After two years of imprisonment, Voynich was sent to Tunka (near Irkutsk in Siberia) but escaped at the end of June 1890, reappearing in London on 5 October of the same year. There he continued political activities, first among Russian immigrants – where he met his wife Ethel Lilian Boole (1864–1960), later a noted novelist – and then in the Polish Socialist Party. Some party members accused him of being a Russian agent, but this seems doubtful. Nevertheless, in 1895 he suddenly gave up politics and became a rare book dealer, soon achieving great international success (Schleinitz 1906/1907, Таратута 1964, Prinke 2006, Prinke and Zandbergen 2007).

THE UNSOLVED ENIGMA OF THE VOYNICH MANUSCRIPT

During World War I, Voynich moved to the USA and for the first time presented the "Roger Bacon Manuscript" (as he called it, accepting Rafael Mnišovský's story) to the general public at the Art Institute of Chicago Exhibition in 1915. In 1919 he invited William Newbold (1865–1926), professor of philosophy at the University of Pennsylvania, to help him decipher the codex. Two years later Voynich and Newbold published their preliminary findings concerning the history of the manuscript, based on enquiries in Prague and the opinions of several authorities (Voynich 1921, Newbold 1921). Also in 1921, Newbold gave great publicity to the manuscript through a series of lectures at various American universities, which were reported by many newspapers and magazines, thus bringing the discovery within the scope of popular culture.

When Voynich died in 1930, his "Cipher Manuscript" was inherited by his wife, and on her death in 1960 she left it to Anne Nill, her lifelong friend and Voynich's former business assistant. Nill sold it a year later to the antiquarian book dealer Hans P Kraus for the sum of US$24,500. Kraus offered the manuscript for sale at US$160,000 but, unable to find a buyer, he eventually donated it to the Beinecke Rare Book and Manuscript Library at Yale University in 1969, where it was catalogued under the call number MS 408.

Studies and decipherment claims

As mentioned above, the first known attempt to decode the Voynich Manuscript was by Jiří Bareš (Georgius Barschius) in the mid-17th century. According to Johannes Marci in his letter to Athanasius Kircher in 1665, Bareš "put untiring work into its decipherment" and "did not give up this hope until he reached the end of his life" (Neal 2000–2010). Marci included the working materials and possibly attempted translations in the same package as the manuscript itself, but these documents are probably lost. Kircher certainly received them, together with the codex itself, but from his 1639 letter to Théodore Moret (Moretus) it seems obvious he was not especially interested in continuing the efforts of Bareš.

Wilfrid Voynich concentrated his research on the history of the manuscript rather than its decoding. He accepted the information from Marci's letter to Kircher that the author of the codex was Roger Bacon and that it had been owned by Emperor Rudolf II. He also put forward the hypothesis that it was John Dee who brought it to Prague (Voynich 1921). When Voynich met William Newbold in

1919, the latter became fascinated with the content of the manuscript and worked on its decipherment for a number of years. He, too, accepted Bacon's authorship and believed he had found the key to reading the text, which he first presented in an article in 1921, while his more extensive working materials were published posthumously in 1928 (Newbold 1921, 1928). The cipher reconstructed by Newbold was extremely complicated and relied on many transformations of the text and minute details of the script. Newbold's friend John Manly, professor of literature and philology, later published an article definitively disproving both Bacon's authorship and Newbold's decoding procedure (Manly 1921, 1931).

Nevertheless, in 1943 a lawyer named Joseph Feely published another decipherment claim along similar lines. Having become interested in the manuscript after reading Newbold's book, Feely proposed that the language used was a highly abbreviated medieval Latin. The fragments he "translated" dealt with the gynecological observations of a medieval scientist using a microscope, which led him to accept Roger Bacon's authorship because, at the time Feely was writing, Bacon was believed to be the inventor of the microscope (Feely 1943). Like Feely, Leonell Strong (1894–1982), a medical scientist, also found gynecological and sexual content in the manuscript. He concluded that it was written in medieval English using a complex cipher, which combined elements of several Renaissance cryptographers (Strong 1945, Strong and McCawley 1947). Strong even identified the author as Anthony Ascham (Askham) (*circa* 1517–59), a physician, who published a herbal and some astrological works. Critics at the time dismissed Strong's findings on methodological and linguistic grounds, and today we may add a chronological argument: the Voynich Manuscript is certainly over a century older than he supposed.

Around the same time Theodore Petersen (1883–1966), a scholar of Eastern languages at the Catholic University of America, adopted a much more systematic approach. He obtained a photostatic copy of the entire manuscript from Ethel Voynich after her husband's death and made a full transcription in the original alphabet, together with a card index of all words and their concordance. Petersen completed it in 1944 but continued to work on the mysterious codex for the rest of his life. He was a faithful correspondent of Ethel Voynich and Anne Nill, and his letters contain many details of his work, but he never published his results (D'Imperio 1978).

Friedman and the "First Study Group"

Perhaps the most professional attempt at deciphering the Voynich Manuscript was undertaken in 1944 by a group of 16 US wartime cryptologists formed by

William F Friedman (1891–1969). Drawing on their experience of cracking Japanese codes and developing early IBM computers, the team transferred part of Petersen's transcription to punched cards using a transliteration alphabet designed by Friedman. This so-called "First Study Group" worked on the manuscript until 1946 when the team was demobilized. Their preliminary results showed the curious statistical properties of the text but failed to achieve a breakthrough. In 1962–3 Friedman attempted to establish a "Second Study Group" but the US electronics company RCA, which initially agreed to finance the project of extensive computer analysis of the entire text (which needed to be transcribed again), soon withdrew its support (D'Imperio 1978).

Friedman maintained his deep interest in the Voynich Manuscript, developing a theory that it contained an artificial language constructed of logical classes of words and synthetic grammar. He published his theory in 1959 in the form of an anagram in a footnote, but it was later discussed in a report by John Tiltman, a British intelligence officer who had been engaged in the Enigma research at Bletchley Park, and whom Friedman introduced to the Voynich Manuscript in 1950 (Tiltman 1967). The third important Voynich researcher of that period was Prescott Currier, a US naval officer and professional cryptologist, delegated to Bletchley Park in 1941, who closely cooperated with Friedman and Tiltman. He produced a new partial transcription with his own transliteration coding and through computer analysis discovered that there were two underlying languages (dialects or cipher applications), which may have been used by two different scribes. Independent computer analyses were carried out at that time by Jeffrey Krischer, a mathematician and computer scientist at Harvard, who developed a number of novel approaches and statistical tools which were also applied by later researchers (D'Imperio 1978).

Renewed interest in the 1970s

In the 1970s Robert Brumbaugh (1918–92), a professor of medieval philosophy at Yale, proposed a decoding of some individual words and phrases in the codex, as well as a general construction of the text, which he believed had been produced by John Dee or Edward Kelley (or both) in order to impress Rudolf II. In his version of the encoding, all characters depicted numbers, which in turn represented letters, but in a rather complex and ambiguous scheme (Brumbaugh 1974, 1975, 1976, 1977). Brumbaugh concentrated his efforts on the plant drawings, taking inspiration from an earlier work by Hugh O'Neill, who identified some of the plants as American species, which thus dated the manuscript after 1492 (O'Neill 1944). Another Yale professor, William Bennett, used the example of the Voynich

Manuscript in his book on problem solving with computers and was the first to show the low entropy of its text – i.e. that the range of letter combinations was far more limited than in normal languages (Bennett 1976). This proved to be an important discovery for later investigations.

By that time the mysterious manuscript was once again capturing popular imagination and some more fantastic solution claims were put forward, with at least two "translations" of the text. In 1978 John Stojko announced that he had found the key, namely that the underlying language was Ukrainian but written without vowels, and that the text discussed pagan Slavic theology, to which the drawings were completely unrelated. He published his full translation in English, which was, curiously, translated into Ukrainian in 1995 (Stojko 1978). A decade later Leo Levitov presented an ambitious, but equally fantastic, hypothesis that the manuscript was the sole surviving document of the Cathars, written in a secret language based on Flemish (Levitov 1987). His "translation" was – like that of Stojko – severely criticized and discarded by the scholarly community. Another discarded proposal was put forward by Michael Barlow, who argued that the manuscript and Marci's accompanying letter were fakes produced by Wilfrid Voynich himself (Barlow 1986). Later discovery of other letters related to the codex among Kircher's correspondence definitively disproved that possibility.

The capstone of the 1970s period of Voynich Manuscript studies was Mary D'Imperio's monograph *The Voynich Manuscript: An Elegant Enigma* published in 1978 by the US National Security Agency and still regarded as the best summary of what was then known and what strategies had been tried to solve the mystery.

The Voynich Manuscript and the internet

The advent of the internet in the early 1990s opened up new possibilities. A new generation of eminent cryptologists took up the heritage of Friedman, Tiltman and Currier. On 5 December 1991 James Gillogly, a computer scientist and cryptanalyst who had written a chess-playing computer program in 1970 and solved many historical ciphers (including, in 1999, three sections of code from the CIA *Kryptos* sculpture), set up the email discussion list voynich@rand.org. In 1990–94, with James Reeds, professor of mathematics and historian of cryptology, and Michael Roe, another cryptography specialist (who received a doctorate in the field from the University of Cambridge in 1997), Gillogly produced an electronic version of Currier's transcription and made it publicly available. A year later the same group, incorporating also Jacques Guy, an Australian linguist and Easter

Island script researcher, prepared a similar electronic encoding of Friedman's transcription from the "First Study Group" archives discovered by Gillogly.

In 1996 the mailing list was joined by Gabriel Landini, a professor of dental pathology at the University of Birmingham, and René Zandbergen, a space-flight dynamics researcher from the European Space Agency, who initiated the European Voynich Manuscript Transcription Project with the aim of transcribing the whole text again. They developed a new transliteration alphabet (called EVA), and Landini designed a computer font to make the transliterated text pronounceable in English, which became the standard for online Voynich discussions. In 1998 Takeshi Takahashi from Tokyo circulated the second (after Friedman's) transliteration of the entire text and Jorge Stolfi, a Brazilian professor of mathematics and computer science, prepared what became known as "The Interlinear File", incorporating all available transcriptions with extensive comments. It became the basis for numerous computer analyses carried out by the ever-increasing number of subscribers to Gillogly's mailing list, many of them using a piece of software called "monkey", written by Jacques Guy to calculate text entropies of various orders. One more full transcription was made in 2005–6 by Timothy Rayhel (aka Glen Claston, 1957–2014), who joined the group in 1996 and later became convinced that Leonell Strong's proposed solution was essentially correct. His analytical approach identified more character forms and minor differences than the earlier "alphabetic" transcriptions and was also made publicly available and used by many investigators.

At the end of the 1990s, Zandbergen, Landini and Stolfi conducted more intensive research into the historical background of the Voynich Manuscript, in collaboration with Philip Neal, an Oxford University specialist in Latin and medieval German, and Nicholas Pelling, a mathematician, philosopher and author of numerous computer games. The most important discovery they made were Kircher's letters, which shed much new light on the history of the manuscript. In 2000 Rafał T Prinke, a historian of alchemy and esotericism from Poland, joined the mailing list, also contributing some historical findings. The group meticulously documented their research material on the website www.voynich.nu, created by René Zandbergen, which eventually became the best resource on the Voynich Manuscript, an online equivalent of D'Imperio's 1978 book.

21st-century theories and counter-theories

As the original mailing list expanded and numerous other sites and blogs appeared, the number of observations, proposals, hypotheses and statistical studies became so huge that it is impossible to even list them here. The most controversial of the recent solution claims are those of Gordon Rugg and Stephen Bax. The former, a British academic from Keele University, proposed in 2004 that the text was randomly created using a Cardan grille (a grid devised by Girolamo Cardano in the mid-16th century for writing secret messages) and large tables of syllables, and that the probable author was Edward Kelley (Rugg 2004a, 2004b). This theory found support in a statistical study by the Austrian mathematician Andreas Schinner, who also suggested that the underlying text was meaningless (Schinner 2007), but other critics pointed out the circularity and ahistorical assumptions behind Rugg's argument.

In 2014 Stephen Bax, a professor of linguistics at the University of Bedfordshire, rejected the "meaningless hoax" theory. He announced that he had identified 14 characters as simple substitutions for Latin letters and deciphered some common plant names (Bax 2014). Bax relied to some extent on the work of Edith Sherwood, whose identifications of plants in the manuscript were criticized by other researchers, as was her theory that the author was a young Leonardo da Vinci (Sherwood 2003–16). Bax's claims met with even fiercer criticisms and he seems to have softened the strength of his initial proposal.

Over the past decade one researcher, Richard SantaColoma, has made a number of claims about the authorship of the manuscript, most of which were disproved by the dating of the vellum to the early 15th century. He noted some similarity of the drawings of what are generally regarded as pharmaceutical containers to early 17th-century depictions of microscopes, which led him to conclude that the manuscript was a cipher notebook belonging to the Dutch inventor Cornelis Drebbel (1572–1633). SantaColoma later modified his theory, drawing parallels with Francis Bacon's *New Atlantis* (*circa* 1624), before finally deciding that the manuscript was a fake fabricated by Voynich (SantaColoma 2008–16).

In his book *The Curse of the Voynich* (2006), Nicholas Pelling argued that the author could be identified as Antonio Averlino (*circa* 1400–1469), an Italian architect and sculptor, although this was regarded as a far-fetched hypothesis even by Pelling himself (Pelling 2006). However, Pelling is certainly right to refer to a "curse" in his title, judging by the number of serious scholars who have announced their success in deciphering the Voynich Manuscript somewhat prematurely and thus lost at least some of their hard-earned credibility.

Perhaps the most commonly (though far from universally) accepted decoding of any part of the manuscript is of a short note at the very end, on folio 116v, known to the Voynich community as *"michiton oladabas"*. The reading was presented by Johannes Albus at a conference held in the Villa Mondragone in 2012 to celebrate the centenary of the traditional "discovery" of the manuscript by Wilfrid Voynich. The scribbles are in Latin alphabet but they could not be read. According to Albus, it is a recipe for a traditional wound plaster made from a goat's liver, written in abbreviated Latin and medieval German. A small drawing of a goat next to it supports his interpretation, while two words written in the Voynichese script within the body of the recipe should provide the key to further decipherment (Albus 2012). So far, however, this promising finding has not enabled anyone to unlock this text which has been bolted shut for over five centuries.

Special features of the manuscript

While everything in the Voynich Manuscript is intriguing, there are a few undoubted "highlights". These include particularly interesting illustrations, special features of the text, as well as places where there appear to be hints on how to translate the text, or "cribs" as cryptographers call them.

Illustrations

The quality of the herbal illustrations is usually considered to be quite low, but this assessment appears to be based entirely on the very sloppy application of paints and pigments. The outline drawings of the plants are usually made quite carefully and with some detail. Why would someone spend a considerable amount of money on parchment, and clearly a lot of time on drawing the illustration outlines and writing the text, only to almost ruin the manuscript with sloppy painting? Some researchers have suggested that the colours were added by a later owner. We propose that the painting may still be the work of the original scribe or draughtsman, but possibly done some years later when he was at an advanced age and gradually losing his eyesight.

While most herbal illustrations cannot be identified with any certainty, there are a few that look quite realistic. On folio 2v we see what looks very much like a water lily. Water lilies are included in contemporary herbal manuscripts of the *Tractatus de Herbis* tradition, where they are usually drawn less realistically. However, the flower of the plant on this folio looks like a lily, not a water lily. In contrast, there is really no doubt that the flower on folio 9v is some kind of pansy or violet. Interestingly, the flowers have been drawn "upside down". The plant on folio 21r looks like a very realistic representation of common knotgrass. A rather similar version of it may be found in the medieval herbal of Pseudo-Apuleius (Bodleian Library, Ashmole 1431) (Velinska 2010–16).

The plant on folio 35v looks like a tree, with clearly recognizable oak leaves at the top, but the grape-like fruits do not seem to belong there. Very similar illustrations are included in the manuscript copies of the *Tractatus de Herbis* tradition, most particularly the herbal preserved as MS BN Lat. 6823 in the Bibliothèque Nationale in Paris (Zandbergen 2012). In these manuscripts, ivy is twirling around an oak tree, and the similarity is so clear that there can be little doubt that the draughtsman of the Voynich Manuscript was inspired by a drawing from one of these works.

As previously discussed, in 1944 the botanist Hugh O'Neill created something of a stir by identifying some of the plants shown in the Voynich Manuscript as native to the Americas. Although these identifications were far from certain, they led most researchers from this time to believe that the work dated from the 16th century, after Columbus's voyages of discovery in the late 15th century. For example, O'Neill identified the plant on folio 93r as a common sunflower, which was first seen in Europe after Columbus's second voyage to the Americas in 1493 (O'Neill 1944).

Within the astronomical section there is a group of seven small stars (f.68r3). This could well represent the Pleiades, which in many languages is called the "seven stars". There is a wavy line connecting this group to the moon in the centre of the page, and there is a label near the group of stars. This is one of the most obvious "cribs" in the manuscript. One suggested reading is "Taurus", but this is far from convincing.

The zodiac diagrams are of special interest because on the one hand they are clearly recognizable, yet on the other hand they have quite distinctive features. Although some signs, like Pisces and Libra, are completely standard, we find that Cancer is represented by a pair of lobsters, Scorpio looks more like a lizard, and Sagittarius is represented by a human with a crossbow. Recently several amateur Voynich researchers have unearthed a series of German manuscripts from throughout the 15th century that feature quite similar illustrations of Sagittarius (most notably Heidelberg Pal.Germ. 298, Vienna cod. 1842 and Vatican MS Pal.Lat. 1369).

Text

Besides the already mentioned running text in paragraphs and text running around circles, and the many hundreds of labels, there are a few pages containing sequences of words or characters. Of particular interest is the circle on folio 57v, which includes a four-times repeating sequence of the same group of 17 characters. Some of these are common characters in the Voynich script, while others appear nowhere else but here. The meaning of the sequence remains a mystery. The first character on each page is usually larger, similar to initials in other manuscripts, but these characters are from a very small subset of the Voynich alphabet. This suggests that they are not really normal characters, particularly as two of these characters, apart from being used as initials, tend to appear only in the first line of a paragraph. Any attempt to translate the text without taking into account these features is bound to fail.

Translations

We now come to the general question of how to translate the text. Many of the statistical analyses that have been done so far provide us with important information about the properties of the text. In 1976 Prescott Currier clearly identified two "dialects" in the text, which he called languages A and B (Currier 1976). We refer to them as "dialects" because they are not as distinct as two completely different languages. Around the same time, William Bennett's discovery of the low entropy of the Voynich text proved that it is not possible to substitute the Voynich Manuscript text letter by letter and end up with a meaningful text in Latin, English or any other European language. This was further confirmed by the work of Jorge Stolfi, who showed in the late 1990s that the words of the Voynich Manuscript follow a word structure that does not exist in any European language, and is also much more fixed than the structures that do exist in Arabic languages. The only comparable examples that Stolfi could find were the monosyllabic languages of East Asia.

Unfortunately, the scope of this introduction does not allow us to dig more deeply into this fascinating topic. Given all the fruitless efforts to decipher the text, one has to wonder if the Voynich Manuscript might not be meaningless after all. The one certain thing is that translating its text is not just a matter of finding the right table of character substitution, and the right language or dialect.

Conclusion

The Voynich Manuscript was most probably conceived and written in the first half of the 15th century, and now, 600 years later, it is receiving more attention than ever. It continues to attract people all over the world, of all ages and all possible backgrounds. It provokes countless theories about its authorship. Is it the work of extra-terrestrials? The meaningless ramblings of a madman? Or the secret workbook of a historically important figure such as Leonardo da Vinci? Every year we receive many new proposed solutions from countries far and wide.

Clearly, for most researchers the main question about the manuscript is: "What does it say?" An equally interesting question seems to us to be: "How was it done?" This question allows for the possibility that there is no meaning to be derived from it, which would help to explain the main mystery that someone could generate a coded text in the Middle Ages that even modern computer resources cannot crack.

This, then, leads to the final question we will ask here: "Why can't we crack it?" Is it precisely because, as the alternative thinker Terence McKenna suggested, we are collectively looking in the wrong direction and that once we do find the solution, it "will prove trivial, but unexpected in some way" (McKenna 1991)? Is there something in there that our modern minds are no longer capable of seeing?

Acknowledgements

We gratefully acknowledge the assistance we have received from many institutions and individuals during our long and continuing involvement in Voynich Manuscript research. The former include especially the Beinecke Rare Book and Manuscript Library of Yale University, the National Library of the Czech Republic (Clementinum) in Prague, the Historical Archives of the Pontifical Gregorian University in Rome, Rome National Central Library, and the Folger Shakespeare Library in Washington, DC. The founders and members of the online Voynich discussion list were the greatest source of information, instruction and sober criticism, thus proving the power of collective research. They are too numerous to mention here, but we would like to extend our special thanks to Jim Reeds, Gabriel Landini, Philip Neal, Nicholas Pelling and Jorge Stolfi for their particularly valuable contributions. Last but not least, we are indebted to Josef Smolka of the Czech Academy of Sciences for sharing with us his unsurpassed knowledge of the intellectual milieu of Rudolfine Prague.

Bibliography

Albus, Johannes. 2012. "The Manuscript's last page – a recipe". In *Voynich-100 Conference*. Villa Mondragone, Monteporzio Catone, Italy.

Barabe, Joseph G. 2009. "Materials analysis of the Voynich Manuscript". Report to the Beinecke Rare Book and Manuscript Library, 1 April 2009.

Barlow, Michael. 1986. "The Voynich Manuscript – by Voynich?" *Cryptologia* no. 10: 210–16.

Bax, Stephen. 2014. *A Proposed Partial Decoding of the Voynich Script*. Available from: stephenbax.net/

Bennett, William Ralph. 1976. *Scientific and Engineering Problem Solving with the Computer*. Englewood Cliffs: Prentice-Hall.

Brumbaugh, Robert S. 1974. "Botany and the Voynich 'Roger Bacon' manuscript once more". *Speculum* no. 49: 546–8.

Brumbaugh, Robert S. 1975. "The solution of the Voynich 'Roger Bacon' cipher". *Yale Library Gazette* no. 49: 347–55.

Brumbaugh, Robert S. 1976. "The Voynich 'Roger Bacon' cipher manuscript: deciphered maps of stars". *Journal of the Warburg and Courtauld Institutes* no. 39: 139–50.

Brumbaugh, Robert S. 1977. *The World's Most Mysterious Manuscript*. London: Weidenfeld and Nicholson.

Clarke, Mark. 2011. "Colours versus colorants in art history: evaluating lost manuscript yellows". *Revista de História da Arte e Arqueologia, serie W* no. 1: 139–50.

Currier, Prescott H. 1976. "Papers on the Voynich Manuscript". In *New Research on the Voynich Manuscript: Proceedings of a Seminar, 30 November 1976*, edited by Mary E D'Imperio. Washington, DC: privately typewritten manuscript, transcribed by Jacques Guy and Jim Reeds in January 1992.

D'Imperio, Mary E. 1978. *The Voynich Manuscript: An Elegant Enigma*. Fort George G. Meade, MD: National Security Agency/Central Security Service.

Evans, RJW. 1984. "Rudolf II and His World". *A Study in Intellectual History 1576–1612*. 2nd corrected ed. Oxford: Oxford University Press (Clarendon Press).

Feely, Joseph M. 1943. *Roger Bacon's Cipher: The Right Key Found*. Rochester, NY: privately printed.

Fletcher, John E. 1972. "Johann Marcus Marci writes to Athanasius Kircher". *Janus* no. 59: 97–118.

Fletcher, John E, ed. 1988. *Athanasius Kircher und seine Beziehungen zum gelehrten Europa seiner Zeit, Wolfenbütteler Arbeiten zur Barockforschung*, 17. Wiesbaden: Harrassowitz.

Fletcher, John E. 2011. *A Study of the Life and Works of Athanasius Kircher, "Germanus Incredibilis", with a Selection of His Unpublished Correspondence and an Annotated Translation of His Autobiography.* Edited for publication by Elizabeth Fletcher, Aries Book Series, 12. Leiden-Boston: Brill.

Garber, Margaret. 2002. *Optics and Alchemy in the Philosophical Writings of Marcus Marci in post-Rudolphine Prague 1612–1670.* San Diego, CA.

Godwin, Joscelyn. 2009. *Athanasius Kircher's Theatre of the World: His Life, Work, and the Search for Universal Knowledge.* London: Thames & Hudson.

Hodgins, Greg. 2012. "Forensic investigations of the Voynich MS". In *Voynich-100 Conference.* Villa Mondragone, Monteporzio Catone, Italy.

Levitov, Leo. 1987. *Solution of the Voynich Manuscript: A Liturgical Manual for the Endura Rite of the Cathari Heresy, the Cult of Isis.* Laguna Hills, CA: Aegean Park Press.

Líva, Václav. 1937. *Seznamy Pražských Novoměšťanů za Léta 1618–1653.* Prague: privately printed.

Manly, John M. 1921. "The most mysterious manuscript in the world: Did Roger Bacon write it and has the key been found?" *Harper's Monthly Magazine,* 186–97.

Manly, John M. 1931. "Roger Bacon and the Voynich Manuscript". *Speculum* no. 6: 345–91.

McKenna, Terence K. 1991. *The Archaic Revival: Speculations on Psychedelic Mushrooms, the Amazon, Virtual Reality, UFOs, Evolution, Shamanism, the Rebirth of the Goddess, and the End of History.* San Francisco: HarperSanFrancisco.

Neal, Philip. 2000–2010. *Transcriptions and Translations of Kircher Letters Related to the Voynich Manuscript.* Available from: www.voynich.net/neal/index.html

Newbold, William Romaine. 1921. "The cipher of Roger Bacon". *Proceedings of the College of Physicians and Surgeons of Philadelphia* no. 43: 431–74.

Newbold, William Romaine. 1928. *The Cipher of Roger Bacon.* Edited by Roland Grubb Kent. Philadelphia: University of Pennsylvania Press.

O'Neill, Hugh. 1944. "Botanical remarks on the Voynich MS". *Speculum* no. 19: 126.

Pelling, Nicholas. 2006. *The Curse of the Voynich: The Secret History of the World's Most Mysterious Manuscript.* Surbiton: Compelling Press.

Pelzel, Franz Martin. 1773–82. *Abbildungen Böhmischer und Mährischer Gelehrten und Künstler nebst kurzen Nachrichten von ihrem Leben und Wirken.* Prague.

Podlaha, Anton. 1903. "Rafael Soběhrd Mnišovský ze Sebuzína (*1580 †1644)". *Sborník Historického kroužku* no. 4: 13–18.

Prinke, Rafał T. 2006. "Wojnicz Michał". In *Encyklopedia Polskiej Emigracji i Polonii*, edited by Kazimierz Dopierała, 331–2. Toruń: Oficyna Wydawnicza Kucharski.

Prinke, Rafał T. 2012. "History of the Manuscript from Rudolf to Voynich". In *Voynich-100 Conference*. Villa Mondragone, Monteporzio Catone, Italy.

Prinke, Rafał T, and René Zandbergen. 2007. "Najdziwniejszy dokument średniowieczny. Komputerowe próby rozszyfrowania Rękopisu Wojnicza". In *Megabajty Dziejów. Informatyka w Badaniach, Popularyzacji i Dydaktyce Historii*, edited by Rafał T. Prinke. Poznań: Instytut Historii, Adam Mickiewicz University.

Quandt, Abigail. 2015. Private communication.

Roberts, Julian, and Andrew G Watson, eds. 1990. *John Dee's Library Catalogue*. London: The Bibliographical Society.

Rugg, Gordon. 2004a. "An elegant hoax? A possible solution to the Voynich manuscript". *Cryptologia* no. 28 (1): 31–46.

Rugg, Gordon. 2004b. "The mystery of the Voynich Manuscript: New analysis of a famously cryptic medieval document suggests that it contains nothing but gibberish". *Scientific American* no. 291 (1): 104–9.

SantaColoma, H Richard. 2008–16. *New Atlantis Voynich Theory*. Available from: www.santa-coloma.net/voynich_drebbel/voynich.html

Schinner, Andreas. 2007. "The Voynich Manuscript. Evidence of the hoax hypothesis". *Cryptologia* no. 31 (2): 95–107.

Schleinitz, Otto von. 1906/1907. "Die Bibliophilen: W. M. Voynich". *Zeitschrift für Bücherfreunde* no. 10: 481–7.

Schmidl, Johannes. 1754. *Historiae Societatis Jesu Provinciae Bohemiae, pars III, ab anno Christi MDCXVI ad annum MDCXXXII*. Prague.

Sherwood, Edith. 2003–16. Edith Sherwood PhD website. Available from: www.edithsherwood.com/

Skinner, Stephen. 2012. *Key to the Latin of Dr John Dee's Spiritual Diaries (1583–1608)*. Singapore: Golden Hoard.

Smolka, Josef, and Ivo Purš. 2014. "Jakub Horcicky (Sinapius) und seine Nobilitation". *Studia Rudolphina* no. 14: 101–13.

Smolka, Josef, and René Zandbergen. 2010. "Athanasius Kircher und seine erste Prager Korrespondenz." In *Bohemia Jesuitica 1556–2006*, edited by Petronilla Cemus, 677–705. Würzburg: Echter.

Stojko, John. 1978. *Letters to God's Eye: The Voynich Manuscript for the First Time Deciphered and Translated into English.* New York: Vantage Press.

Strong, Leonell C. 1945. "Anthony Askham, the author of the Voynich Manuscript". *Science*, 608–9.

Strong, Leonell C, and EL McCawley. 1947. "A verification of a hitherto unknown prescription of the 16th century". *Bulletin of the History of Medicine* no. 21 (November-December): 898–904.

Svobodný, Petr, ed. 1998. *Joannes Marcus Marci: A 17th-century Bohemian Polymath.* Prague: Charles University Press.

Teige, Josef. 1893. *Úmluva. Příspěvek k diplomatice zápisů Desk zemských Království českého.* Prague: F Bačkovský.

Tiltman, John. 1967. "The Voynich Manuscript: 'The most mysterious manuscript in the world' [2]". *National Security Agency Technical Journal* no. 12: 41–85.

Vacek, František. 1923. "Dějiny Bubenče v letech 1620–1910". *Sborník Příspěvků k Dějinám Hlavního Města Prahy* no. 4: 1–296.

Velinska, Ellie. 2010–16. Voynich Manuscript blog. Available from: ellievelinska.blogspot.com/

Voynich, Wilfrid M. 1921. "A preliminary sketch of the history of the Roger Bacon cipher manuscript". *Proceedings of the College of Physicians and Surgeons of Philadelphia* no. 43: 415–430.

Zandbergen, René. 2012. "Pre-Rudolfine history of the MS". In *Voynich-100 Conference.* Villa Mondragone, Monteporzio Catone, Italy.

Zandbergen, René, and Rafał T Prinke. 2005. "The Voynich MS in Prague, from Rudolf II to Johannes Marcus Marci". *Acta Universitatis Carolinae, Mathematica et Physica* no. 46, Supplementum: 141–52.

Zandbergen, René, and Rafał T Prinke. 2011. "Voynichův rukopis v rudolfínské Praze". In *Alchymie a Rudolf II. Hledání tajemství přírody ve střední Evropě v 16. a 17. století,* edited by Ivo Purš and Vladimír Karpenko, 297–314. Prague: Artefactum.

Zimmern, Helen. 1908. "The romance of a literary treasure-house". *Pall Mall Magazine.*

Таратута, Евгення. 1964. *Этель Лилиан Войнич: Судьба писателя и судьба книги.* 2nd ed. Moscow: Художественная литература.

THE
VOYNICH
MANUSCRIPT

Notes on navigating the manuscript

When referring to particular pages in the manuscript, we have followed the Beinecke Rare Book and Manuscript Library principle of using the folio number followed by an r for "recto" when we have needed to specify the front of the folio, or a v ("verso") for the reverse. For the foldout folios, we have added an extra number – 1, 2 or occasionally 3 – to identify the individual parts of the foldout. On pages that show subsections of a foldout folio, we also display a photograph of the extended folio (recto or verso side). As an additional aid to navigation, we have included diagrams that show how each folio is bound into the manuscript's remaining 18 quires (sets of folded sheets or bifolios).

Some folios were removed from the manuscript during the course of its long history. The missing folios are as follows:

☀ folio 12, apparently cut out, stub still visible;

☀ folios 59–64, three bifolios that should have been in the centre of quire 8;

☀ folio 74, cut out, stub still visible (cut marks are clearly visible on folio 75r);

☀ quire 16, which appears to have consisted of one bifolio composed of folio 91 and folio 92;

☀ quire 18, which appears to have consisted of one bifolio composed of folio 97 and folio 98;

☀ folios 109 and 110, which should have been in the centre of quire 20.

Front cover

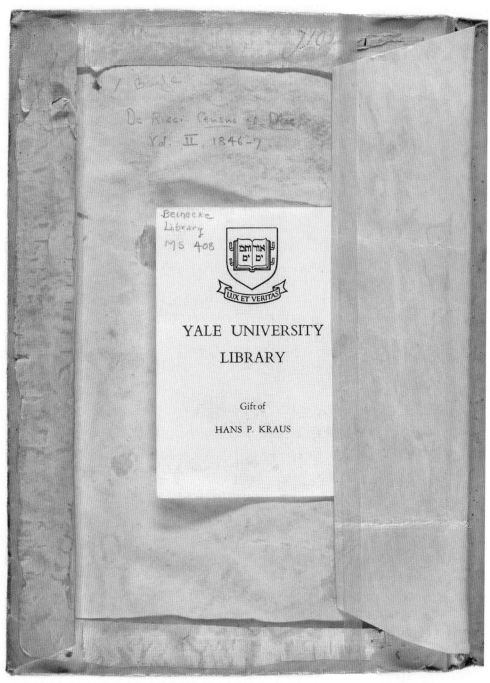

☀ *Inside front cover*

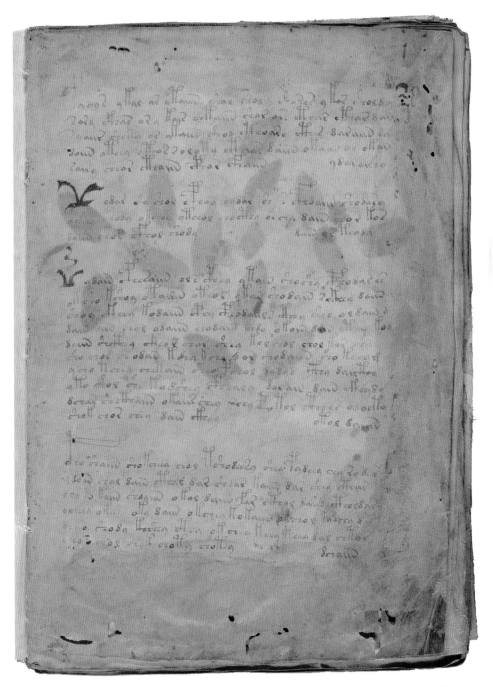

☀ *f.1r*

Quire 1

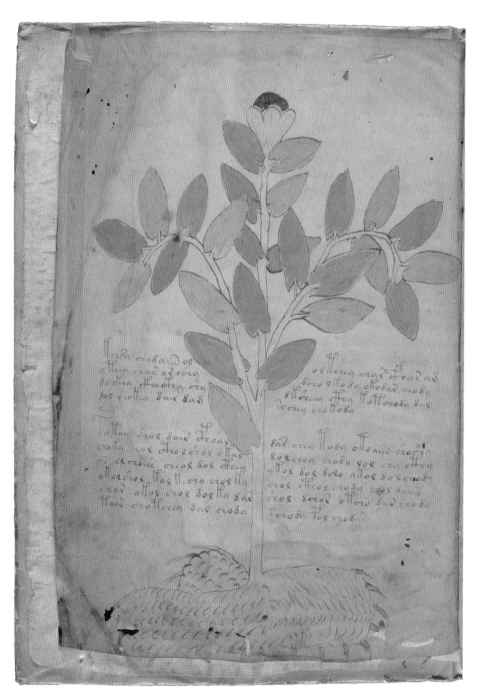

f.2r

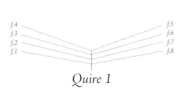

Quire 1

f.2v

☀ f.3r

Quire 1

f.4r

Quire 1

f.5r

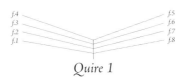

Quire 1

☀ f.6r

Quire 1

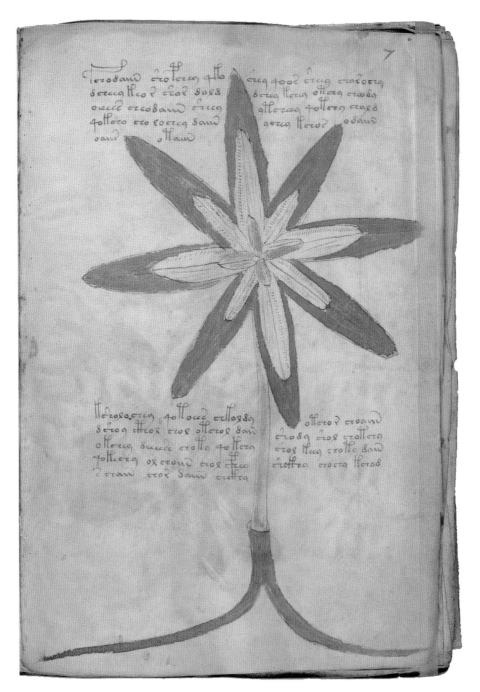

☀ f.7r

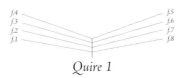

Quire 1

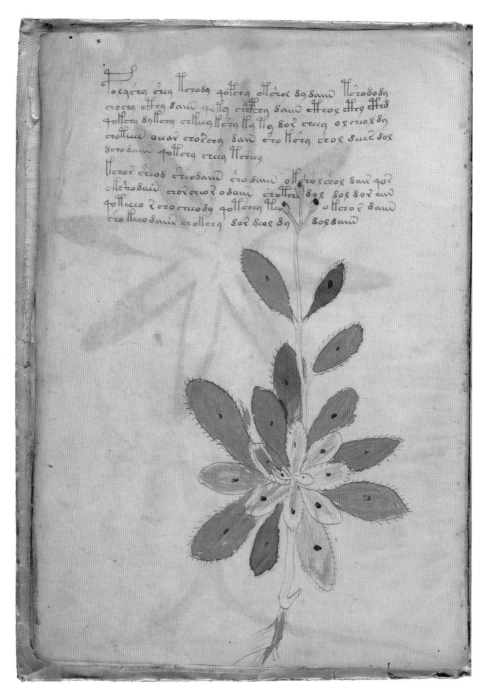

f.7v

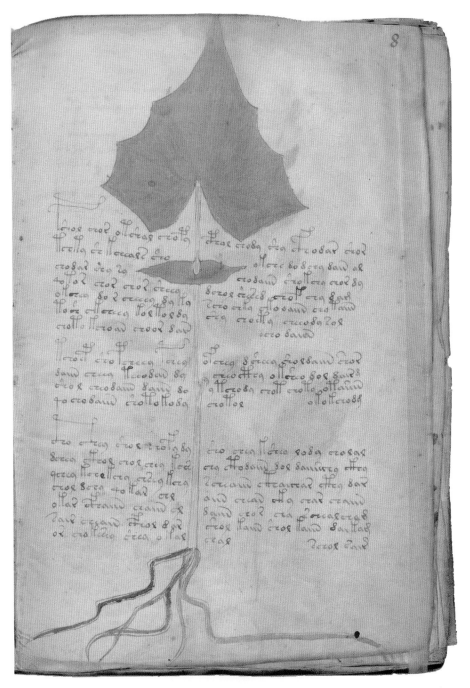

☀ *f.8r*

Quire 1

☀ f.9r

Quire 1   Quire 2

f.9v

Quire 2

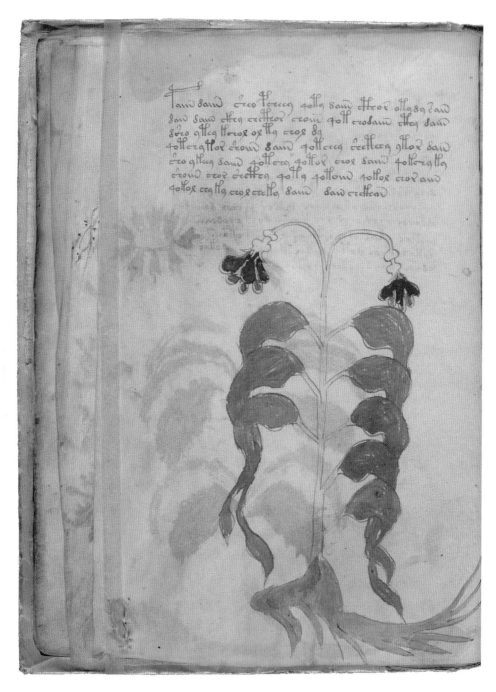

f.10v

☀ *f.11r*

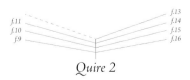

Quire 2

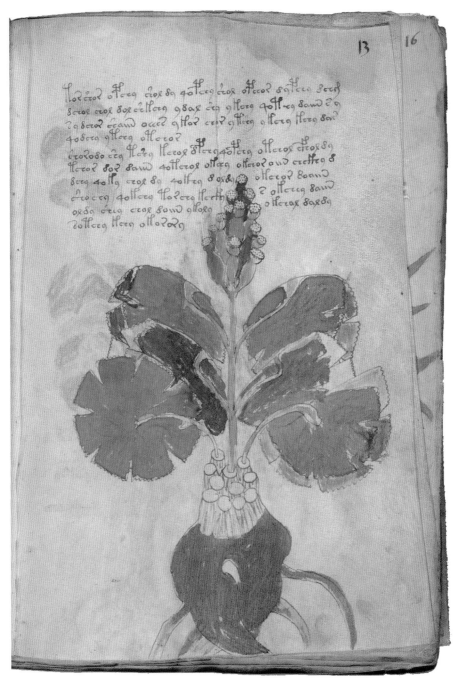

f.13r

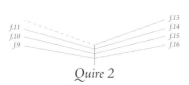

Quire 2

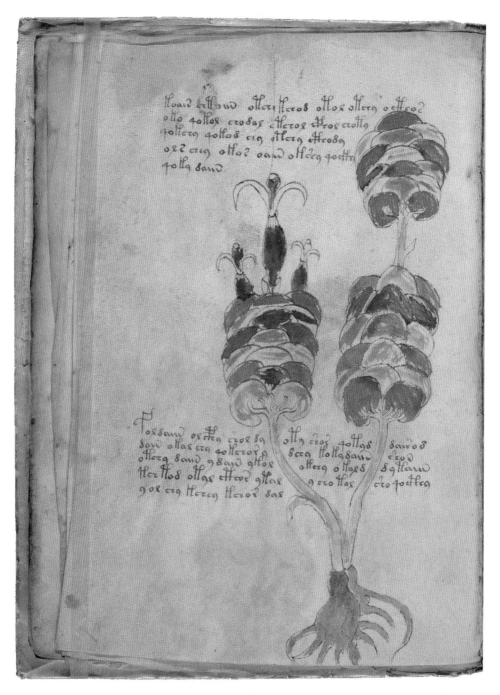

14   16

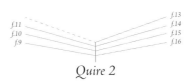

☀ f.14r

f.13
f.14
f.11   f.15
f.10   f.16
f.9

Quire 2

f.15r

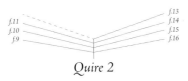

Quire 2

16

f.13
f.14
f.11   f.15
f.10   f.16
f.9

Quire 2

f.16v

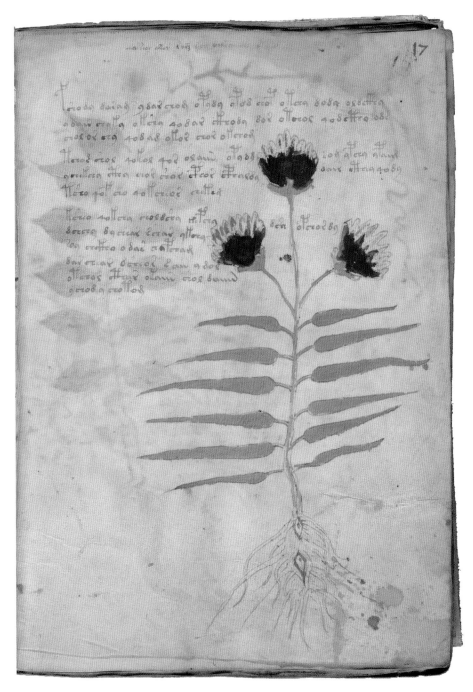

☀ *f.17r*

Quire 2   *Quire 3*

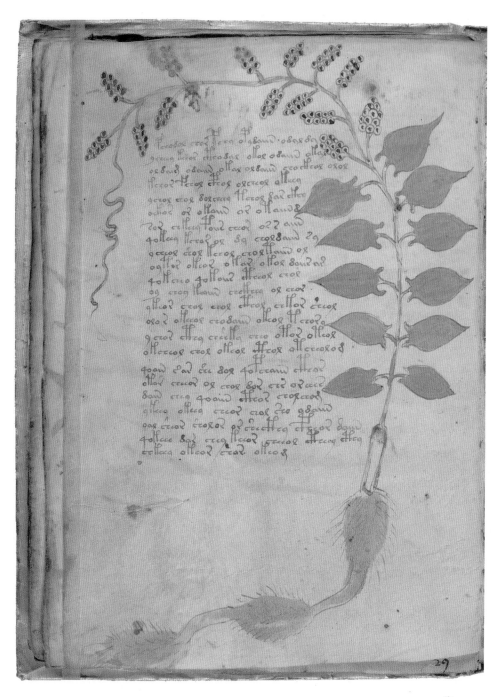

f.17v

18

f.18r

Quire 3

f.19r

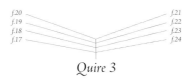

Quire 3

f.19v

f.20r

☀ *f.21r*

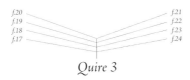

Quire 3

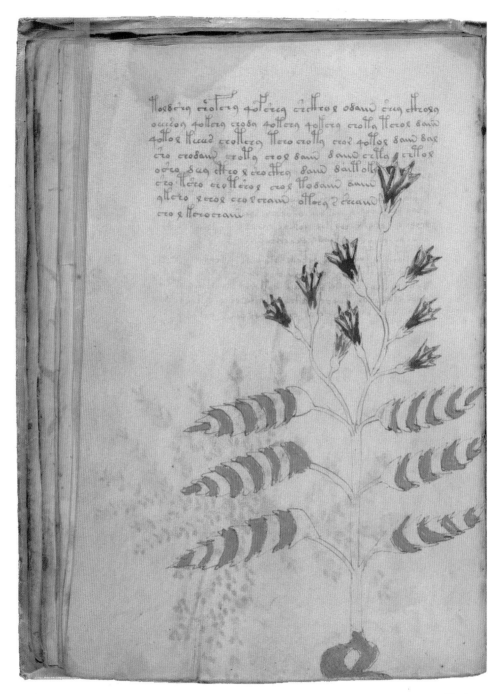

f.20
f.19
f.18
f.17

f.21
f.22
f.23
f.24

Quire 3

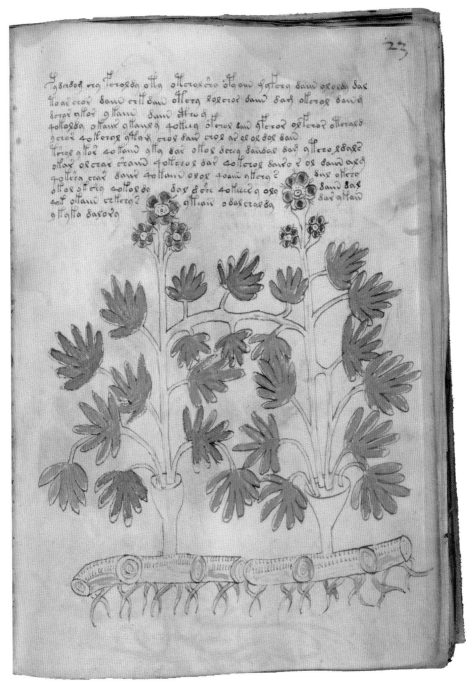

☀ *f.23r*

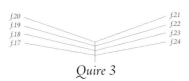

Quire 3

f.23v

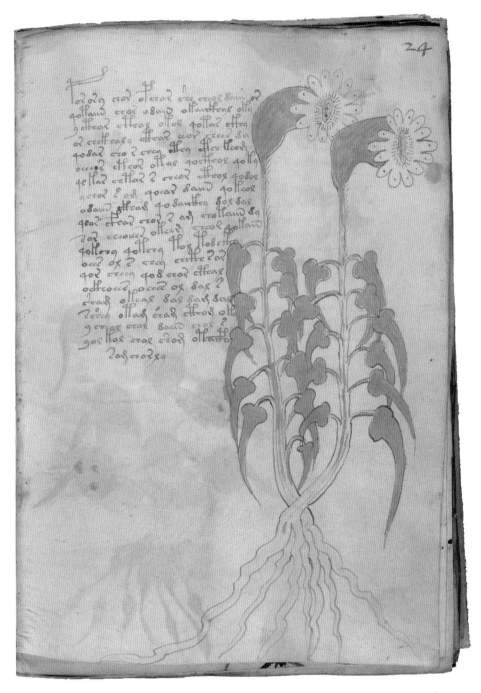

Quire 3

f.24v

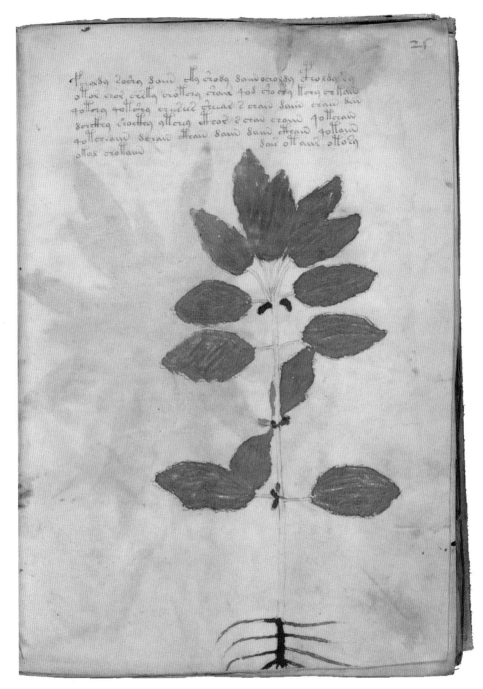

✹ *f.25r*

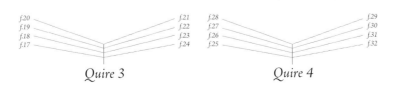

f.25v

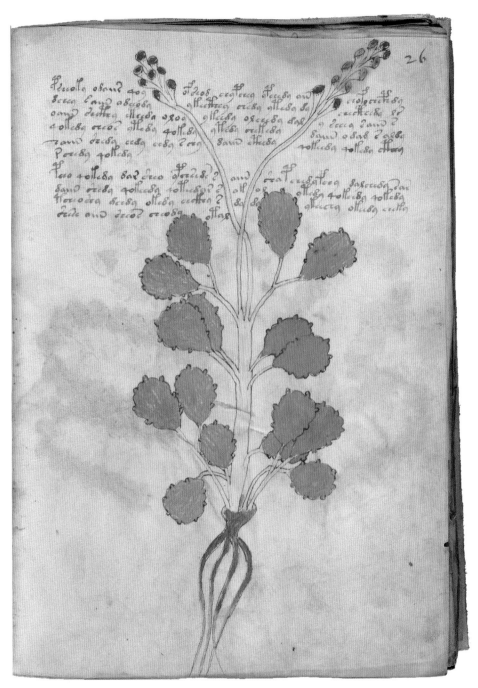

f.26r

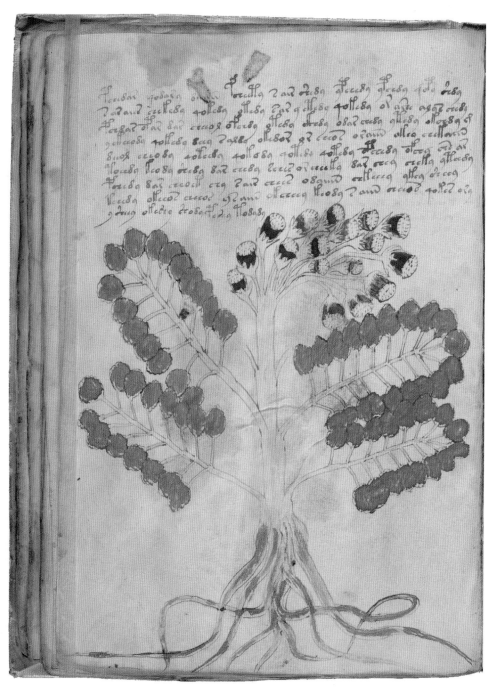

f.26v

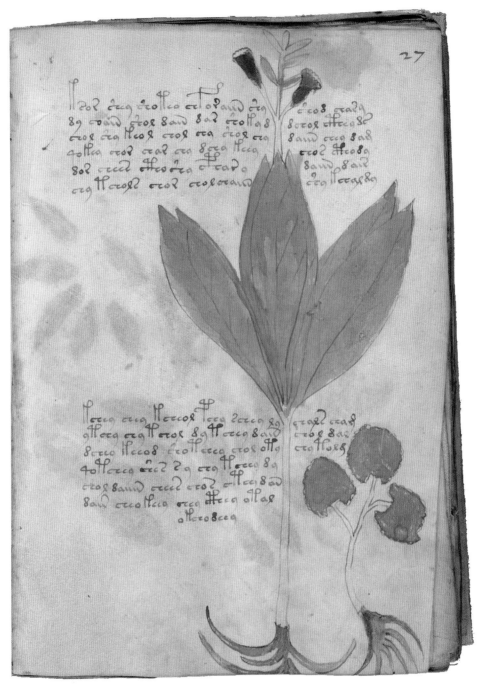

☀ f.27r

Quire 4

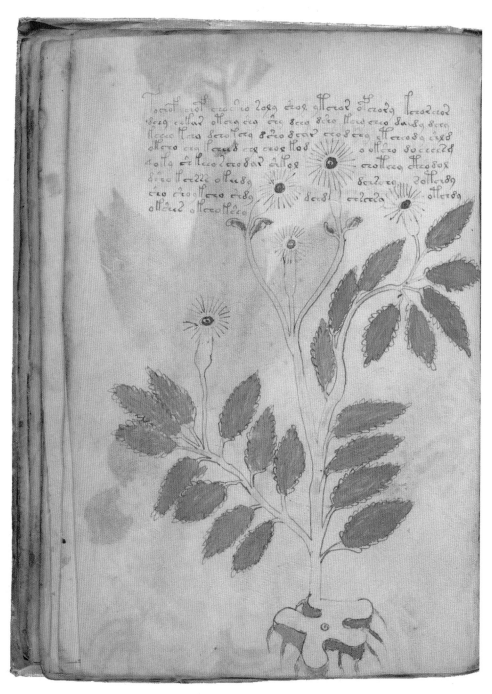

☀ *f.27v*

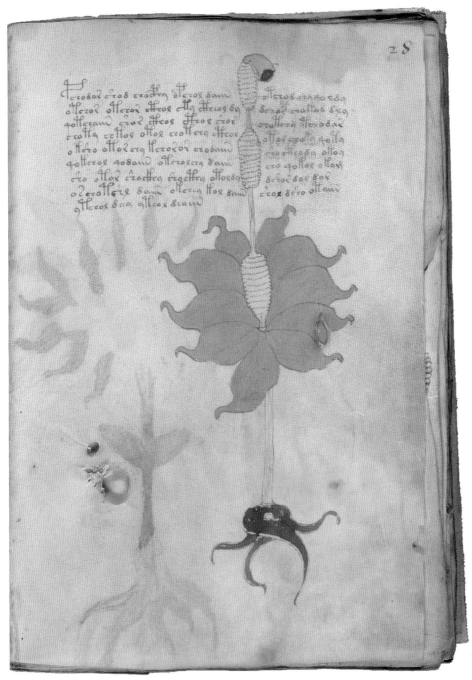

f.28r

Quire 4

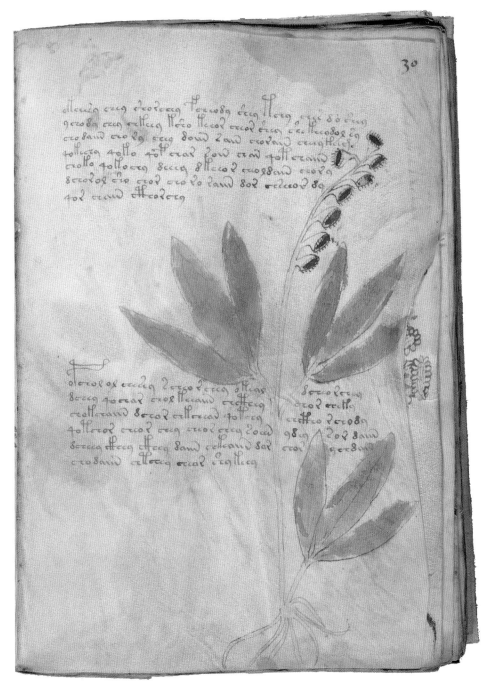

Quire 4

f.30v

31

☀ f.31r

Quire 4

f.31v

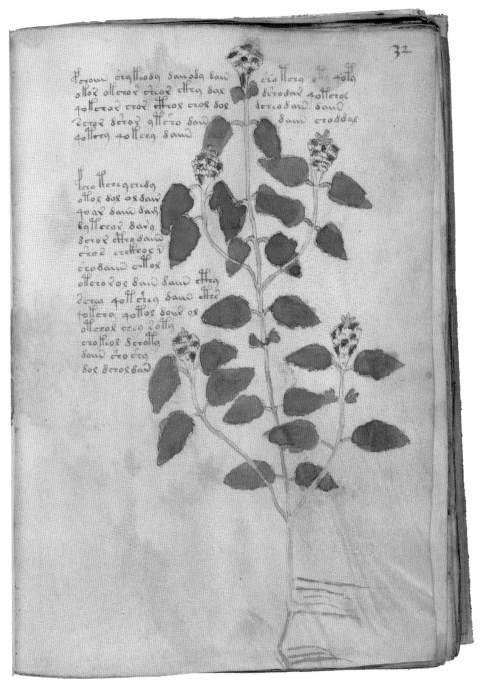

f.32r

Quire 4

f.32v

f.33r

f.33v

34

Quire 5

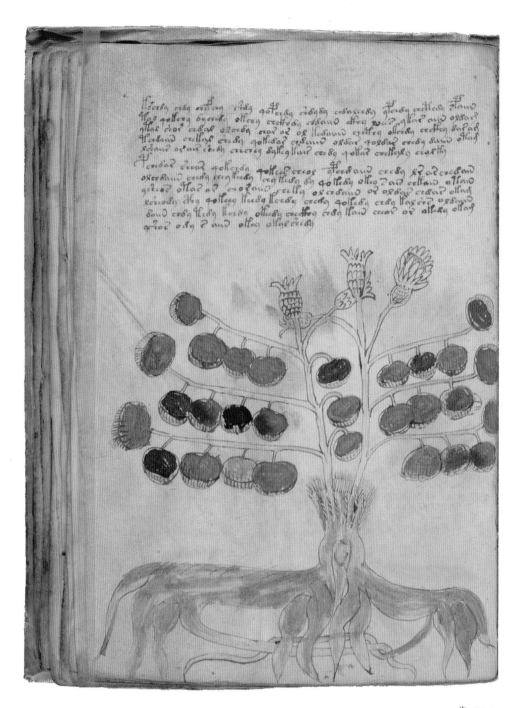

f.34v

35

☀ f.35r

Quire 5

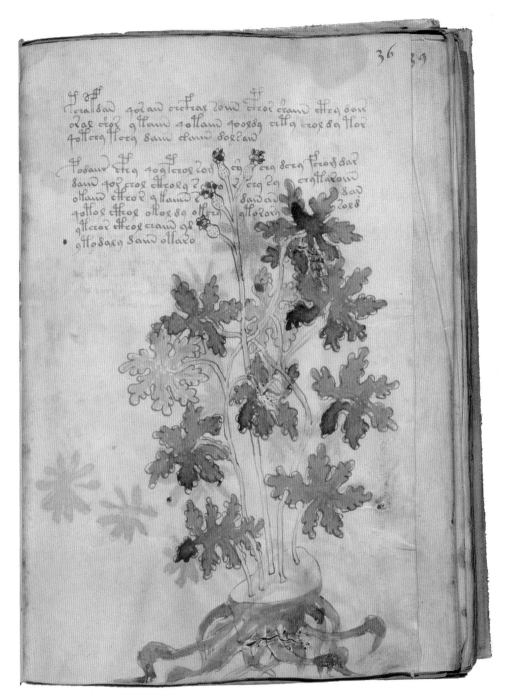

☀ f.36r

Quire 5

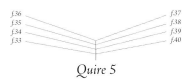

Quire 5

f.37v

f.38r

Quire 5

Quire 5

f.39v

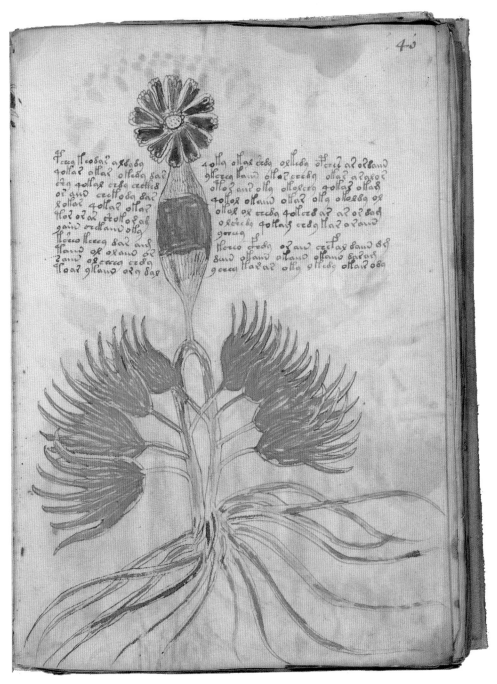

☀ f.40r

Quire 5

f.40v

☀ *f.41r*

f.41v

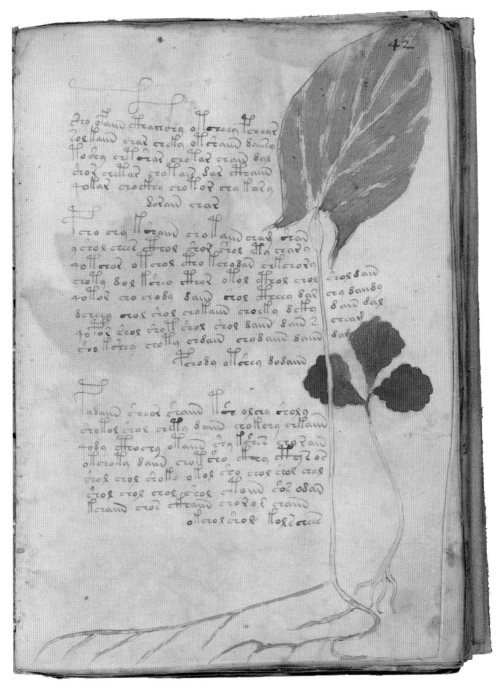

☀ f.42r

Quire 6

f.43r

f.43v

☀ f.44r

f.44
f.43
f.42
f.41
f.45
f.46
f.47
f.48

Quire 6

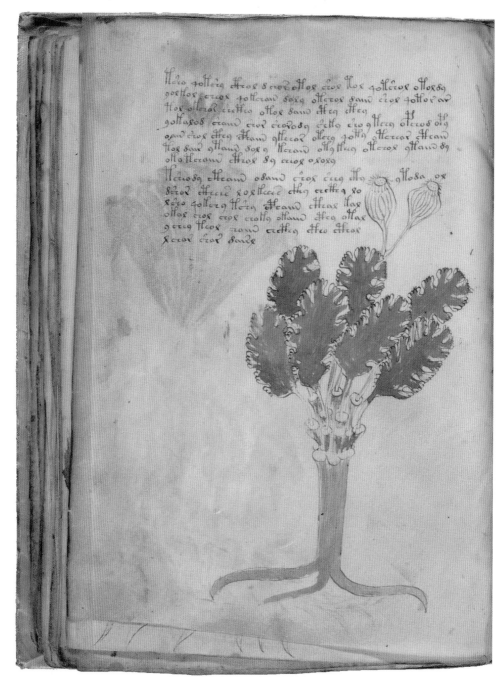

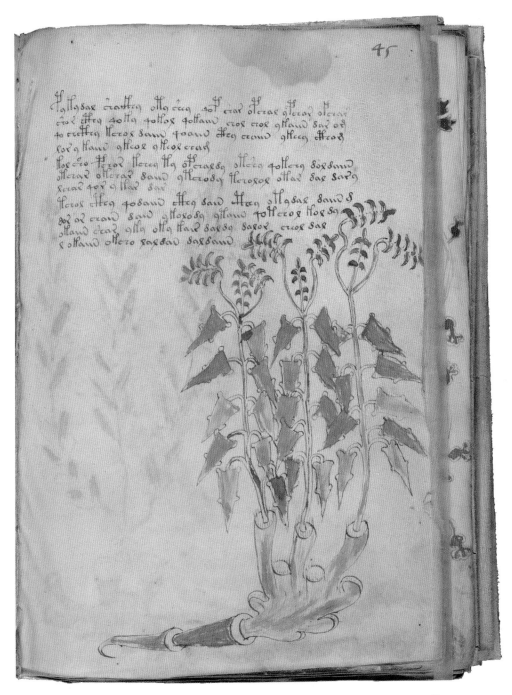

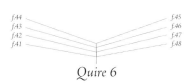

Quire 6

f.45v

☀ f.46r

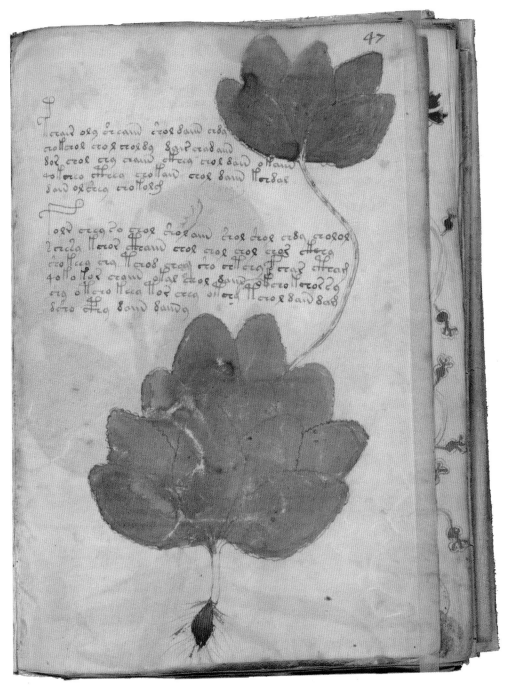

☀ *f.47r*

Quire 6

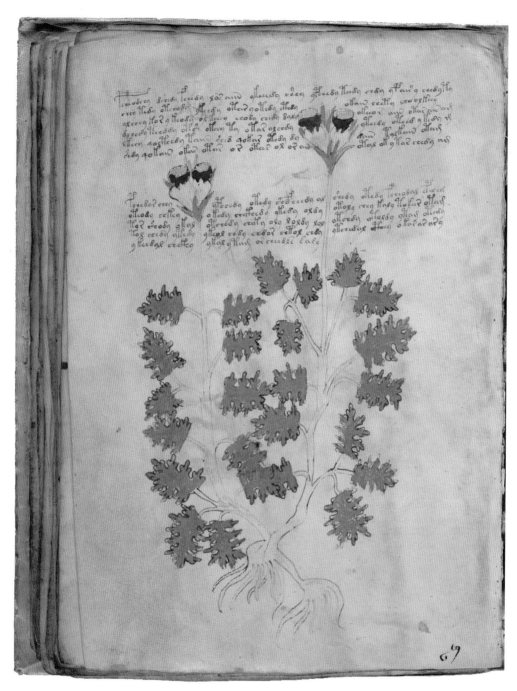

☀ f.49r

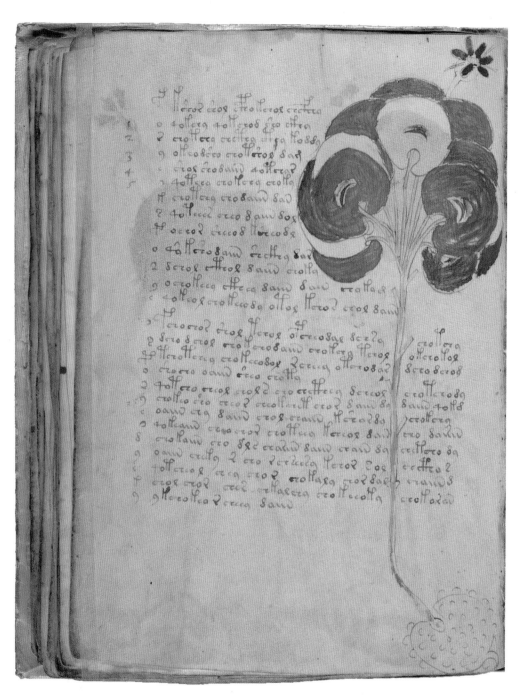

f.50r

Quire 7

f.50v

f.51r

Quire 7

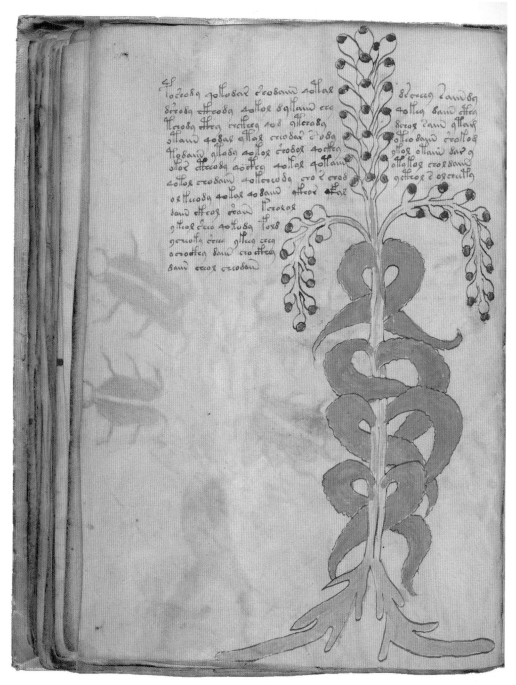

f.52r

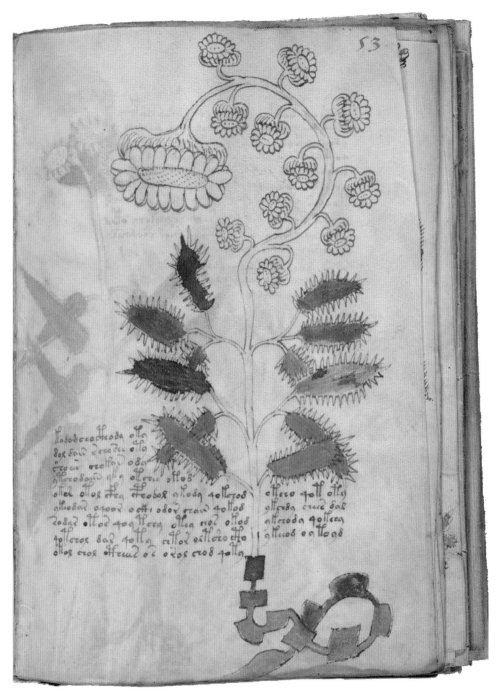

☀ f.53r

Quire 7

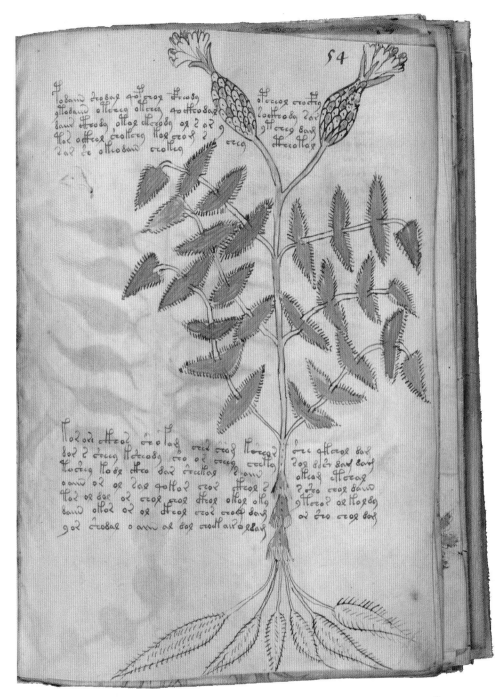

f.52
f.51
f.50
f.49

f.53
f.54
f.55
f.56

Quire 7

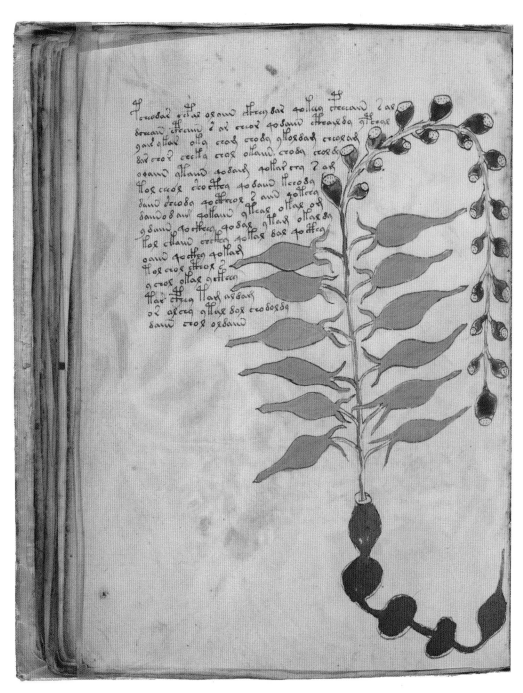

55

Quire 7

f.55v

56

f.56r

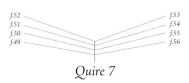

f.52   f.53
f.51   f.54
f.50   f.55
f.49   f.56

Quire 7

☀ f.57r

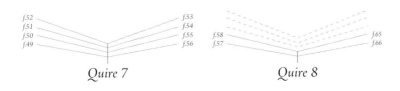

☀ *f.57v*

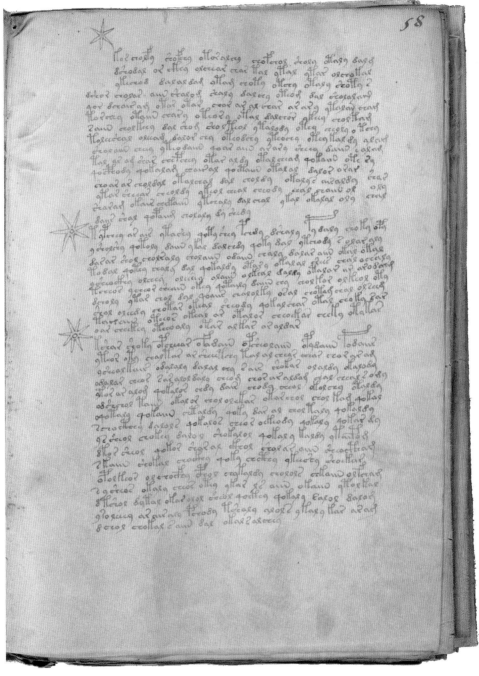

58

☀ f.58r

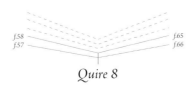

f.58   f.65
f.57   f.66

Quire 8

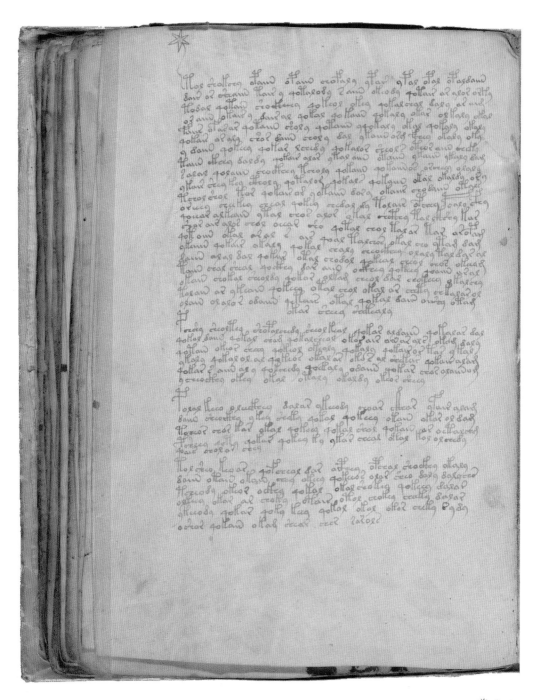

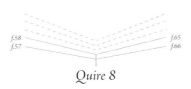

Quire 8

f.65v

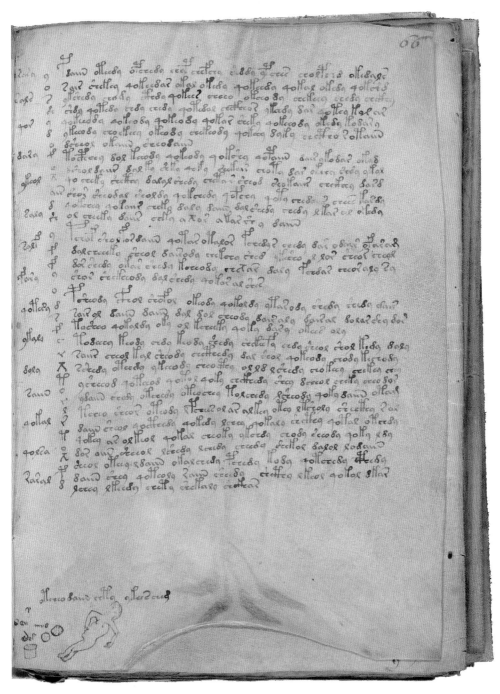

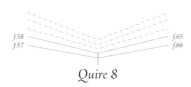

☀ f.66r

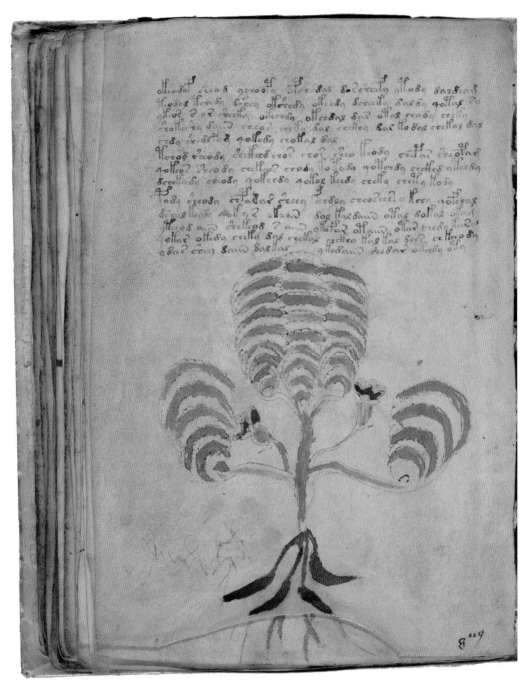

☀ *f.66v*

f.66v   *f.67r1*   *f.67r2*

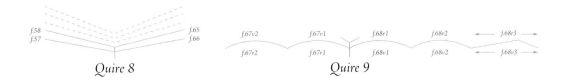

f.67r1

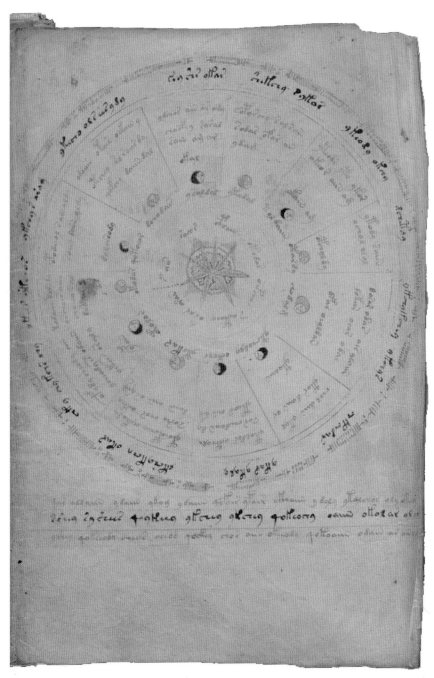

☀ *f.67r2*

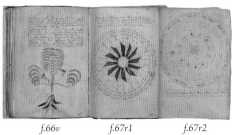

f.66v   *f.67r1*   *f.67r2*   *f.67v2*   *f.67v1*   *f.68r1*   *f.68r2*   *f.68r3*

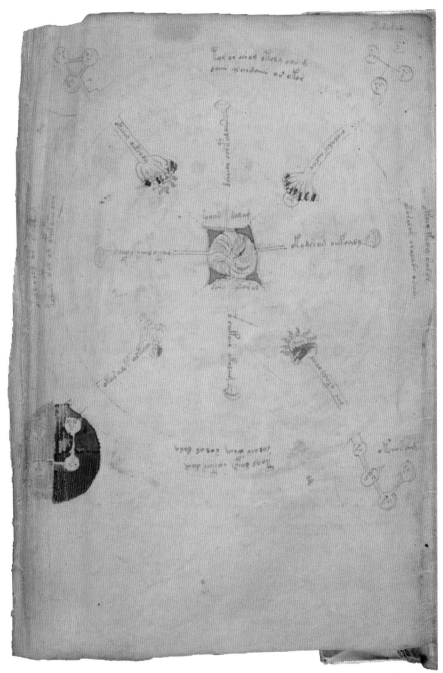

☀ *f.67v2*

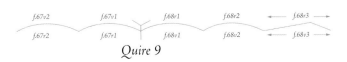

Quire 9

f.67v1

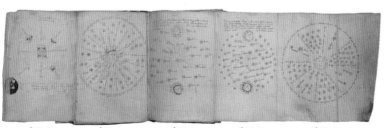

f.67v2   f.67v1   f.68r1   f.68r2   f.68r3

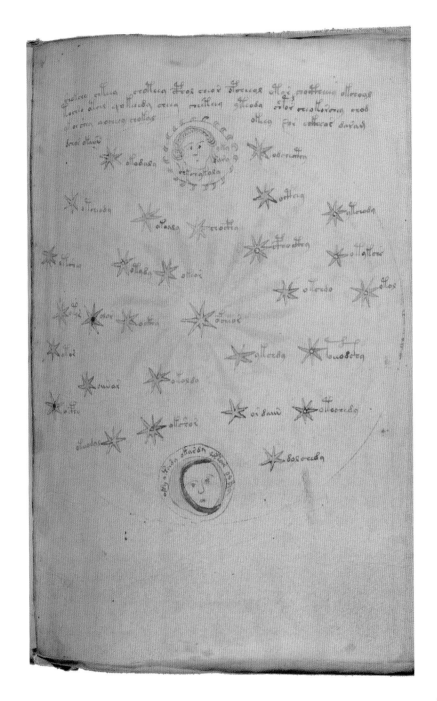

☀ *f.68r2*

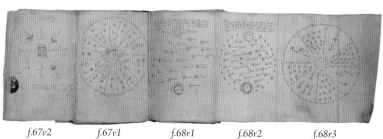

f.67v2   *f.67v1*   *f.68r1*   *f.68r2*   *f.68r3*

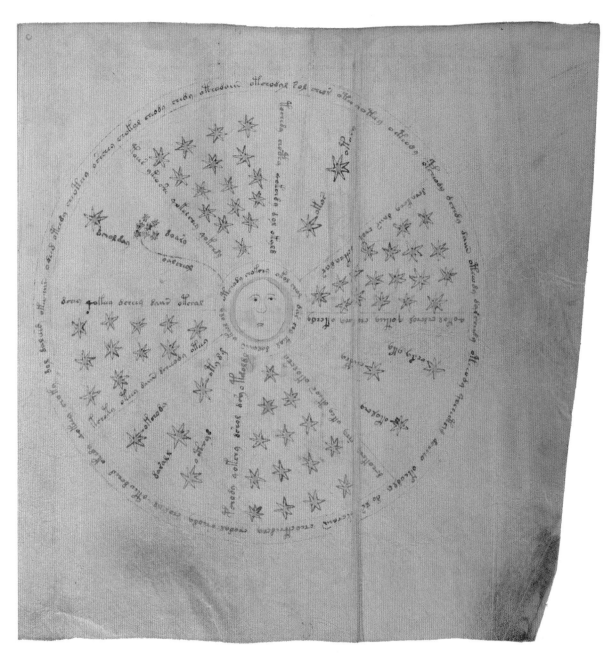

f.68r3

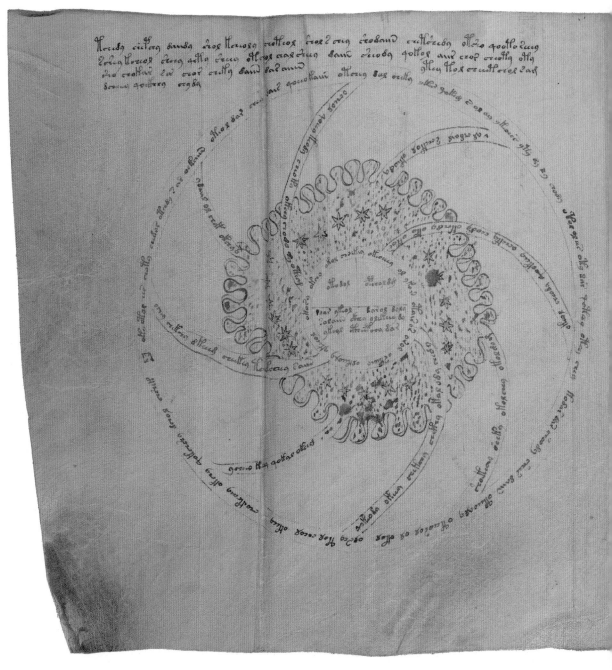

☀ f.68v3

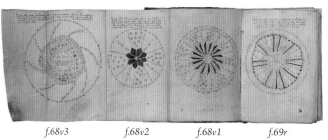

f.68v3　　　　f.68v2　　　　f.68v1　　　　f.69r

f.68v2

❋ *f.68v1*

f.68v3   *f.68v2*   *f.68v1*   *f.69r*

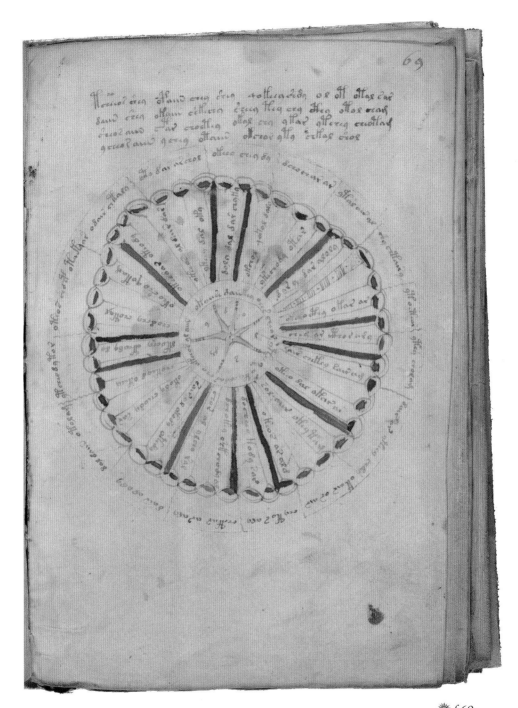

☀ *f.69r*

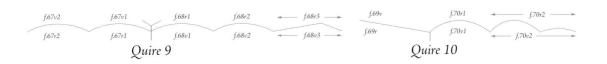

 f.69v

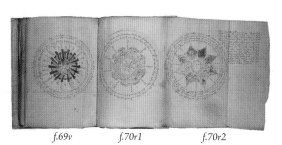

f.69v   f.70r1   f.70r2

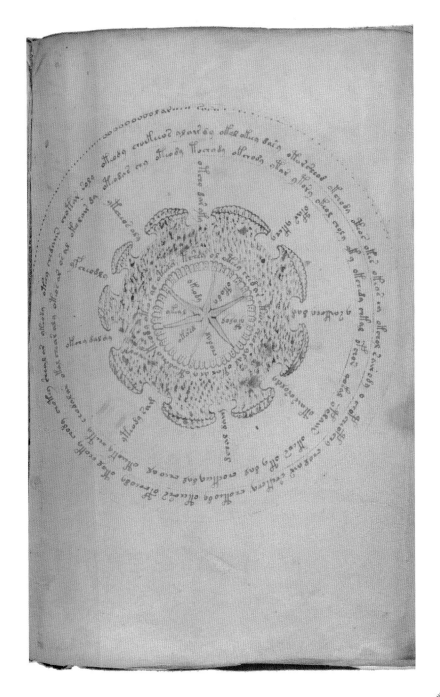

☀ *f.70r1*

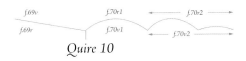

Quire 10

 f.70r2

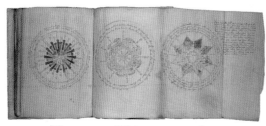

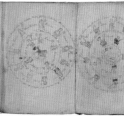

f.69v   *f.70r1*   *f.70r2*   *f.70v2*   *f.70v1*   *f.71r*

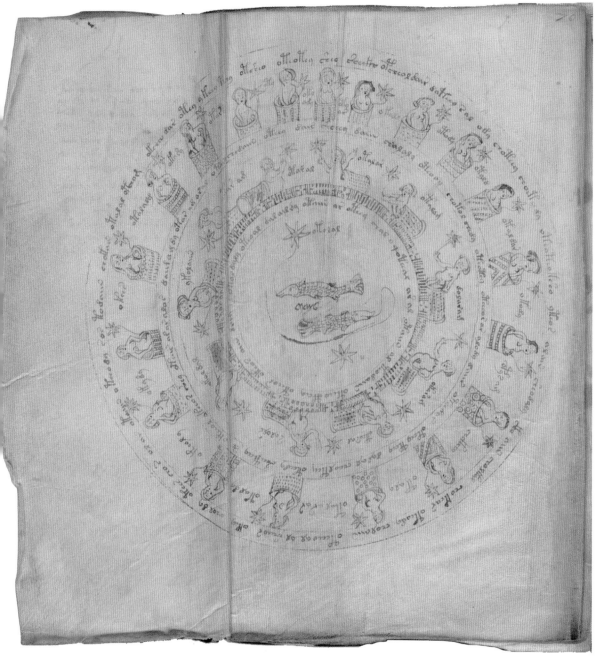

☀ *f.70v2*

Quire 10

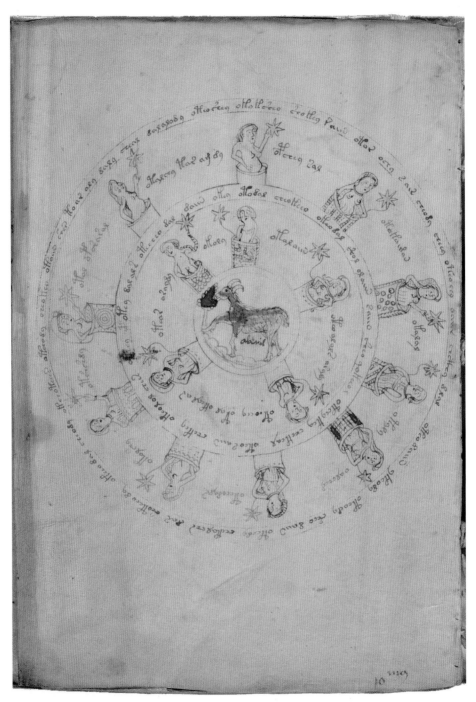

☀ *f.70v1*

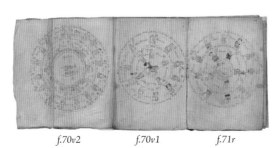

f.70v2   *f.70v1*   *f.71r*

71

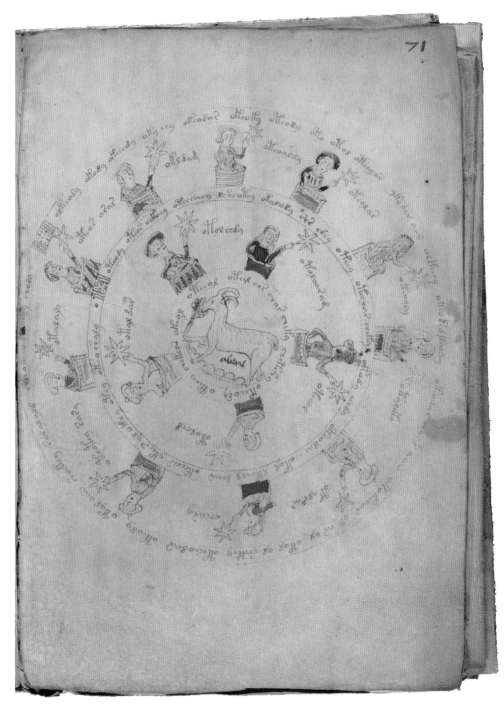

☀ f.71r

Quire 10 *Quire 11*

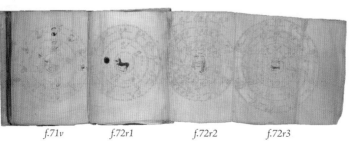

f.71v   f.72r1   f.72r2   f.72r3

☀ *f.72r1*

Quire 11

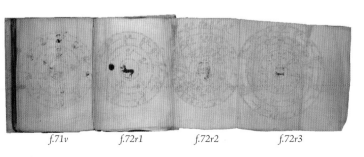

f.71v   f.72r1   f.72r2   f.72r3

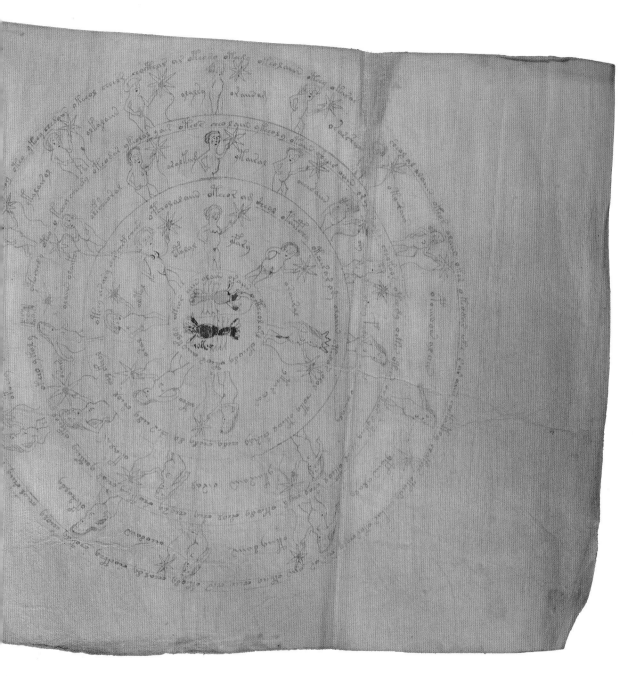

☀ f.72r3

Quire 11

☀ *f.72v3*

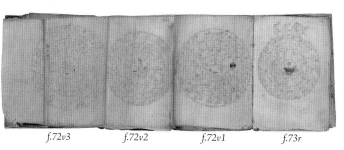

f.72v3   *f.72v2*   *f.72v1*   *f.73r*

☀ *f.72v2*

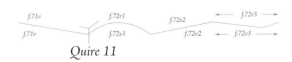

Quire 11

☀ f.72v1

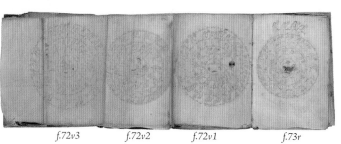

f.72v3   f.72v2   f.72v1   f.73r

✸ *f.73r*

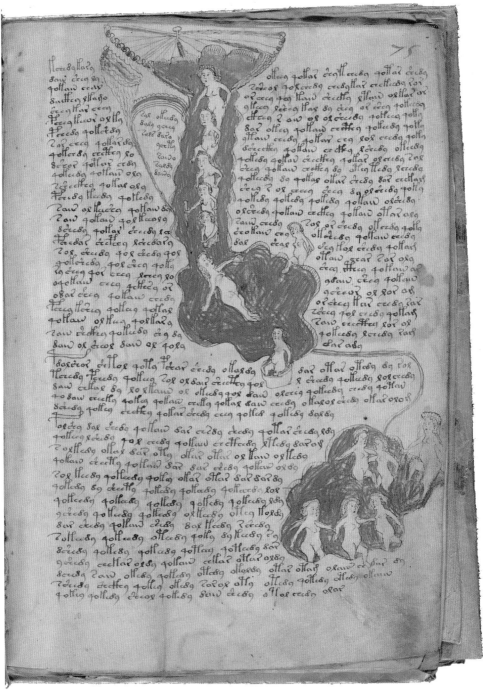

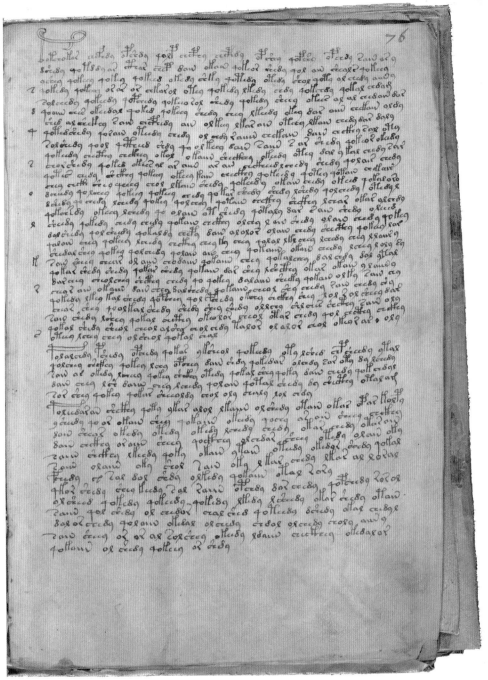

f.76r

Quire 13

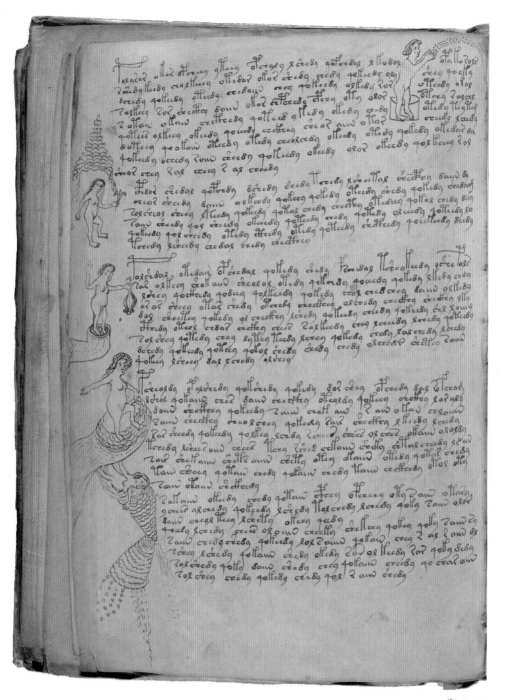

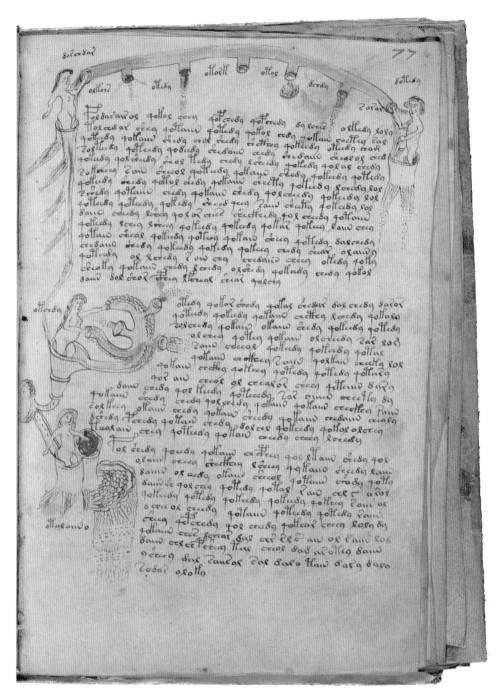

Quire 13

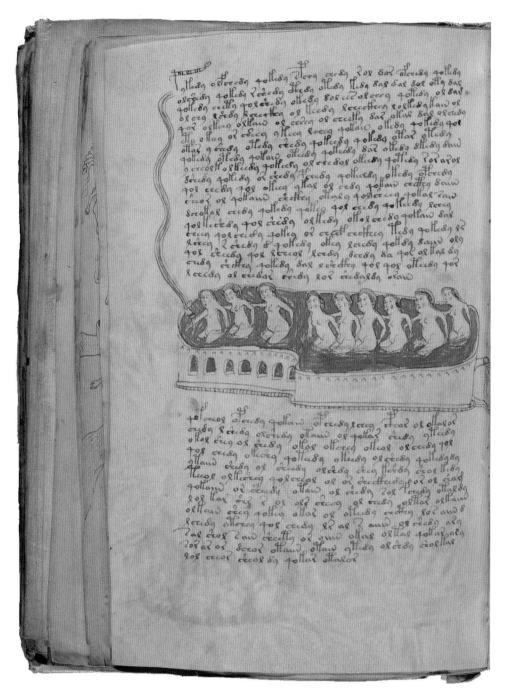

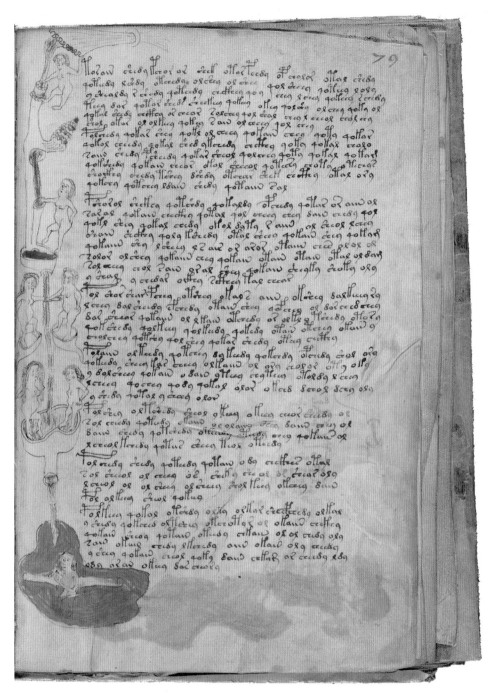

79

 f.79r

f.79 f.80
f.78 f.81
f.77 f.82
f.76 f.83
f.75 f.84

Quire 13

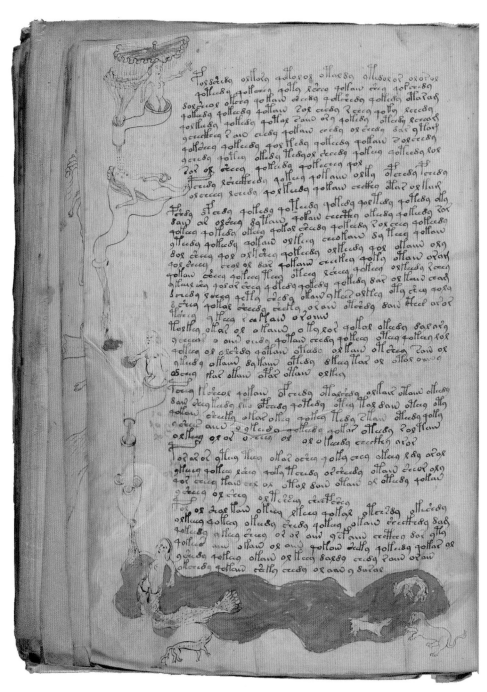

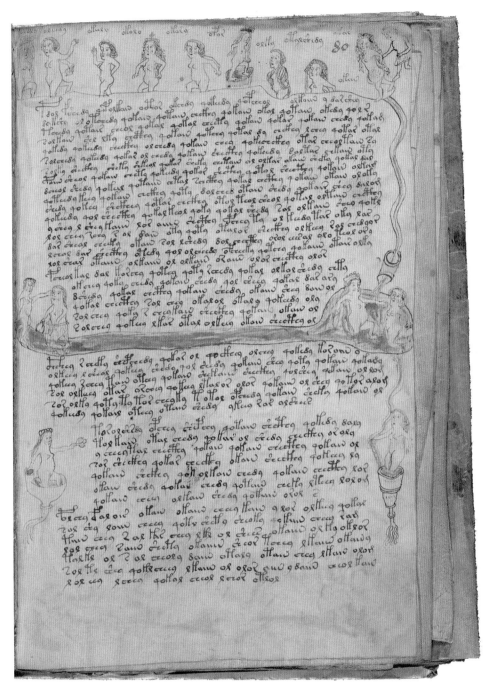

Quire 13

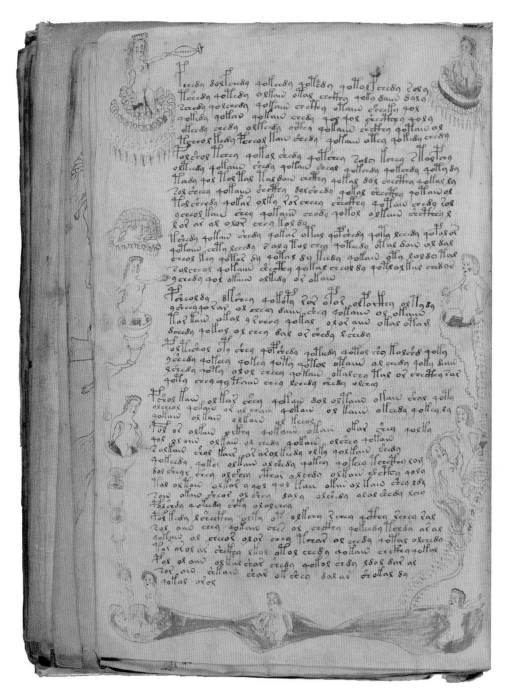

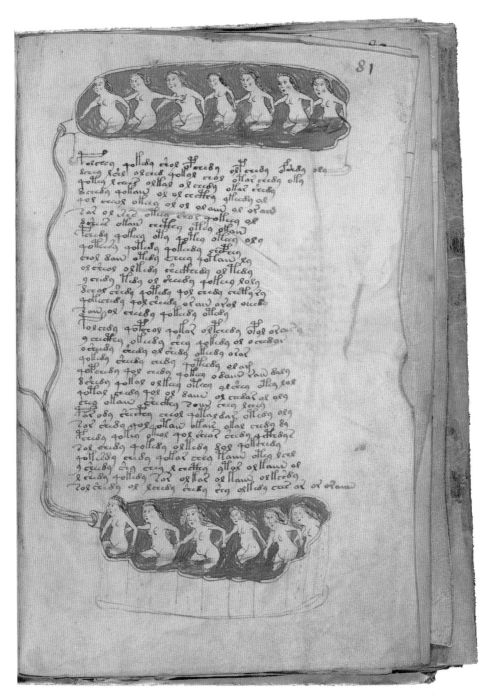

Quire 13

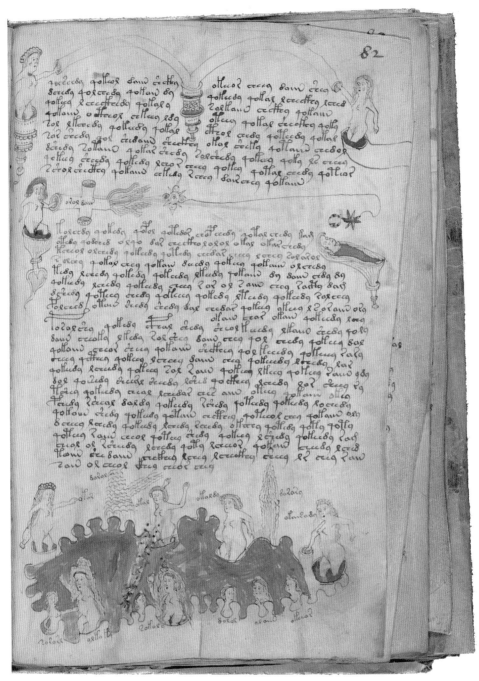

82

☀ f.82r

Quire 13

Quire 13

f.84r

Quire 13

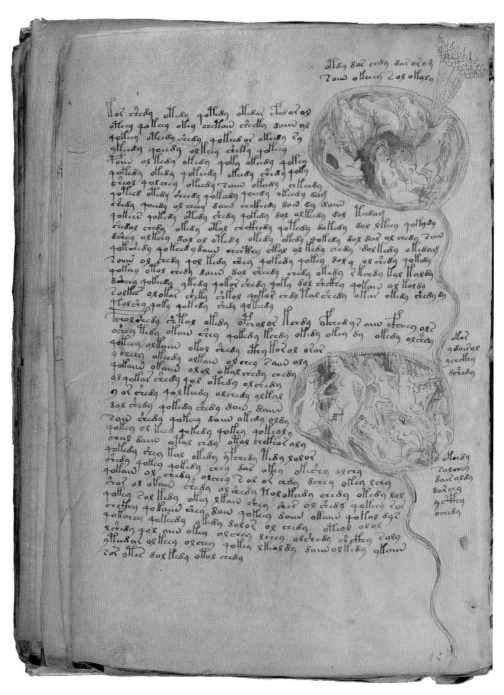

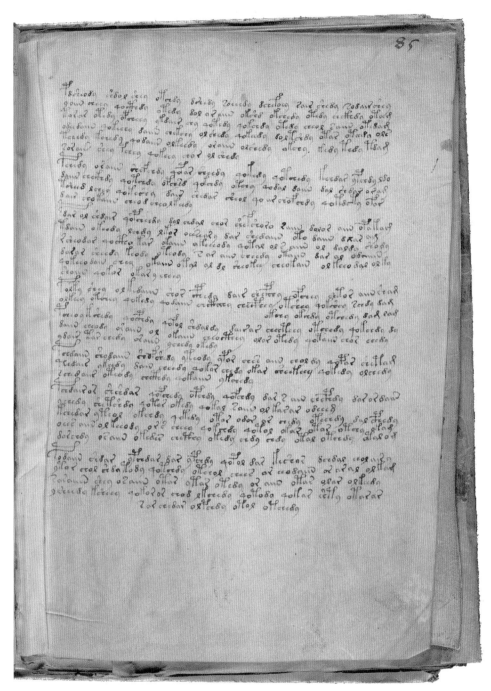

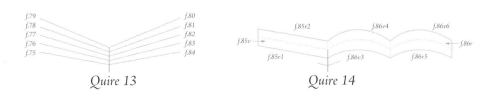

☀ f.85r2

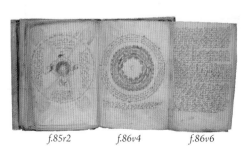

f.85r2   f.86v4   f.86v6

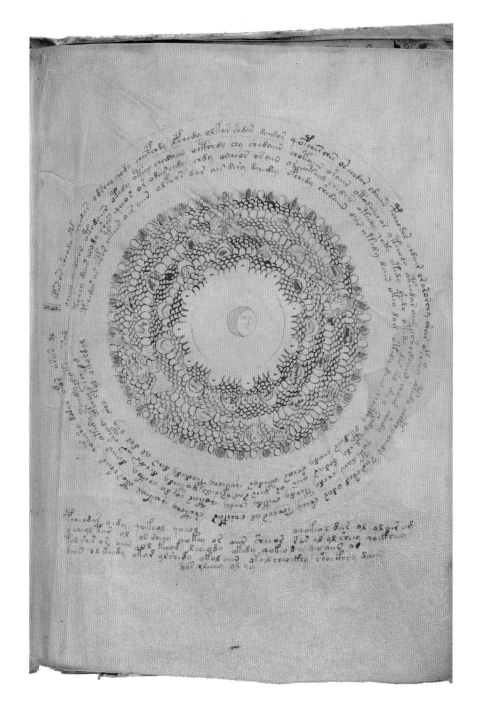

☀ f.86v4

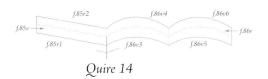

Quire 14

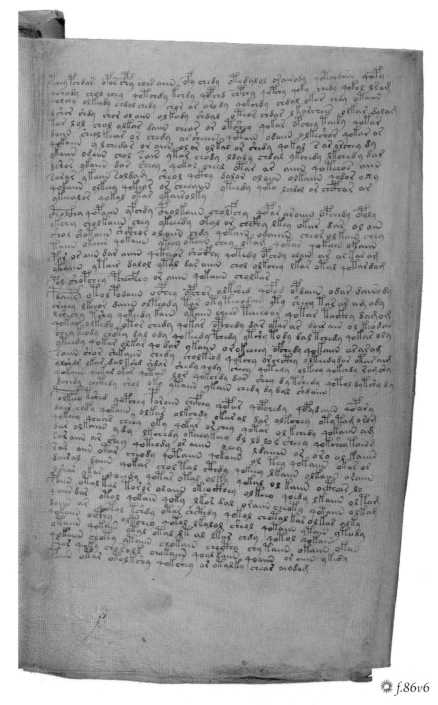

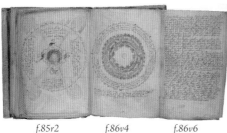

f.86v6

f.85r2   f.86v4   f.86v6   f.86v5   f.86v3   f.87r

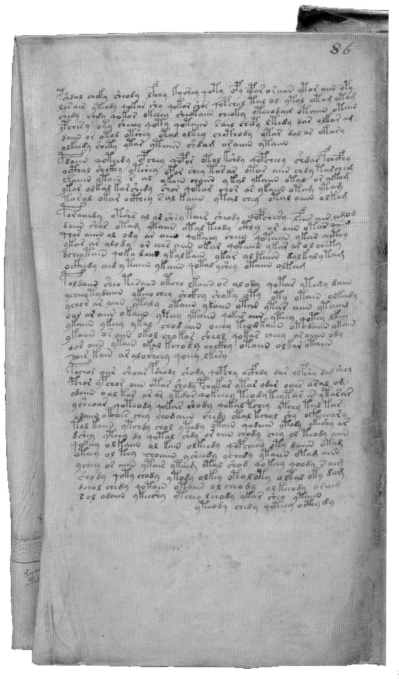

86

☀ f.86v5

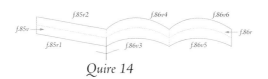

Quire 14

✹ *f.86v3*

f.86v5   *f.86v3*   *f.87r*

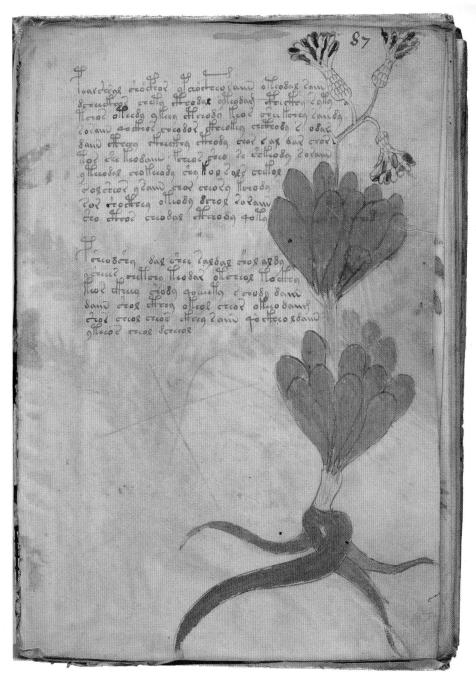

f.87r

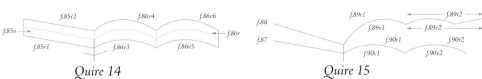

Quire 14

Quire 15

☀ *Overview of the "Rosettes" page*

☀ *f.85v*

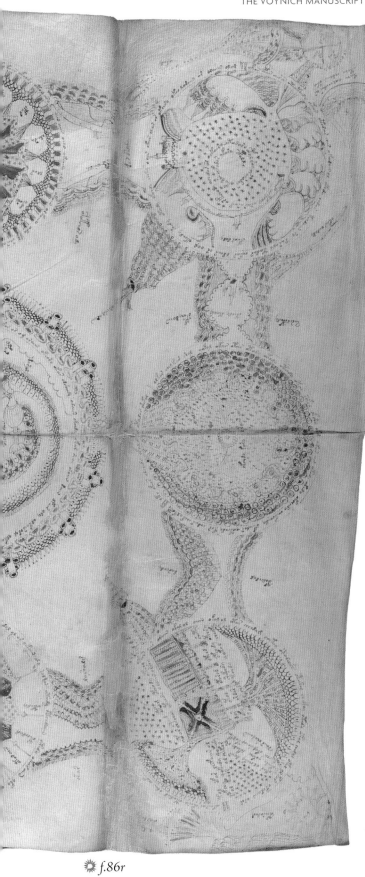

☀ *f.86r*

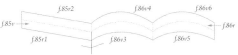

Quire 14

☀ *f.85v (bottom left of "Rosettes" page)*

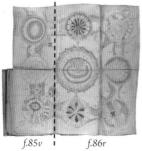

f.85v | *f.86r*

☀ *f.86r (bottom centre of "Rosettes" page)*

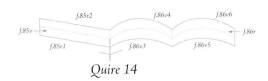

Quire 14

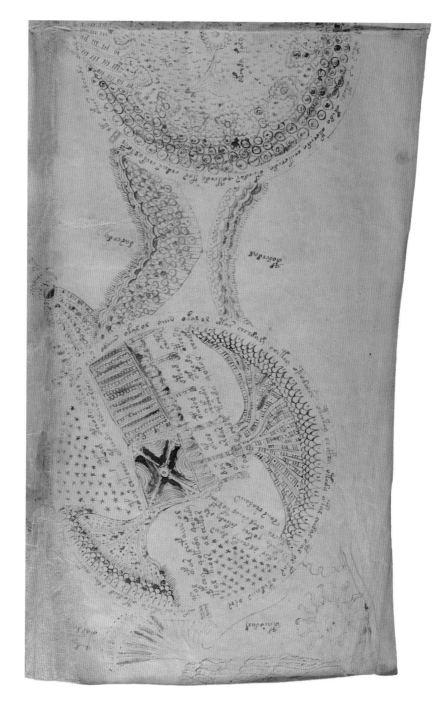

f.86r (bottom right of "Rosettes" page)

f.85v *f.86r*

☀ *f.86r (upper right of "Rosettes" page)*

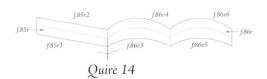

Quire 14

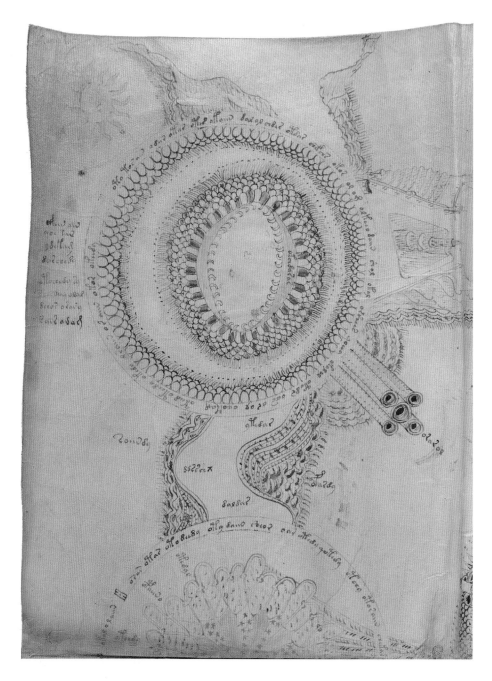

☀ *f.85v (upper left of "Rosettes" page)*

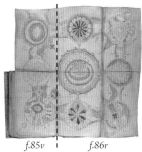

f.85v   f.86r

☀ *f.86r (upper centre of "Rosettes" page)*

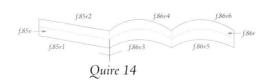

Quire 14

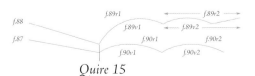

Quire 15

f.88v

f.88v   f.89r1   f.89r2

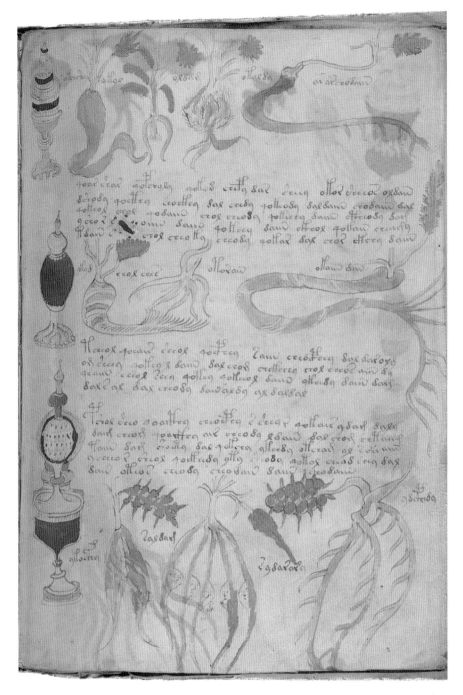

✺ *f.89r1*

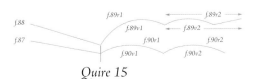

Quire 15

☀ *f.89r2 (part)*

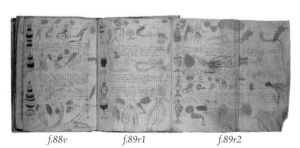

f.88v   *f.89r1*   *f.89r2*

❋ *f.89r2 (part)*

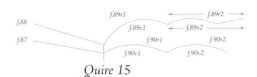

Quire 15

☀ *f.89v2 (part)*

f.89v2   *f.89v1*   *f.90r1*   *f.90r2*

☀ *f.89v2 (part)*

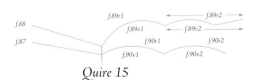

Quire 15

☀ *f.89v1*

f.89v2　　　　*f.89v1*　　　　*f.90r1*　　　　*f.90r2*

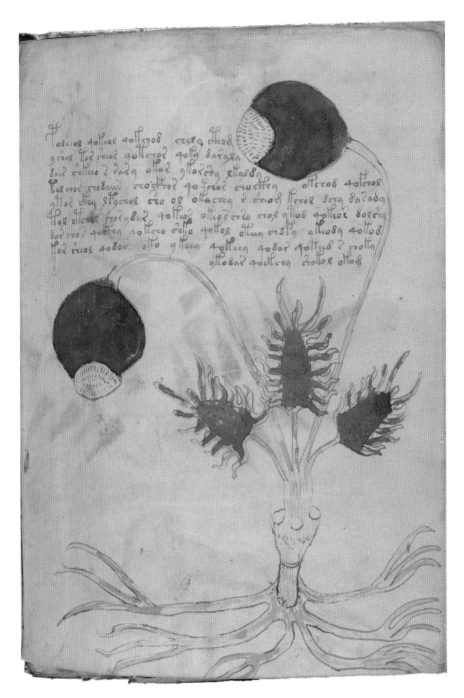

☀ *f.90r1*

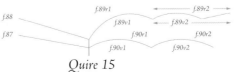

Quire 15

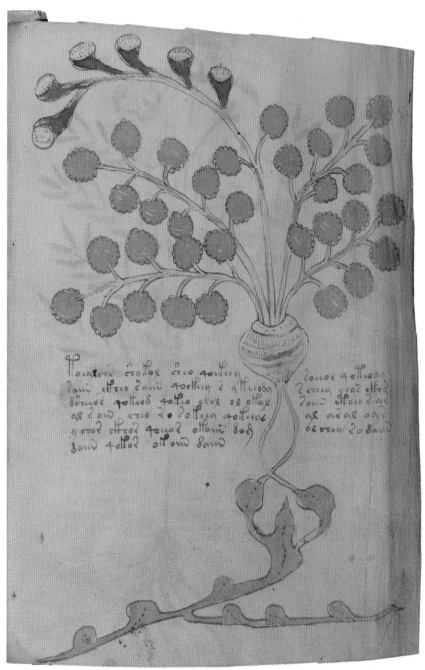

☀ *f.90r2*

f.89v2 *f.89v1* *f.90r1* *f.90r2* *f.90v2* *f.90v1* *f.93r*

f.90v2

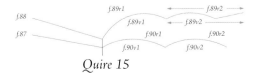

Quire 15

f.90v1

f.90v2   f.90v1   f.93r

f.93r

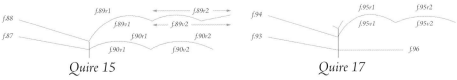

Quire 15   Quire 17

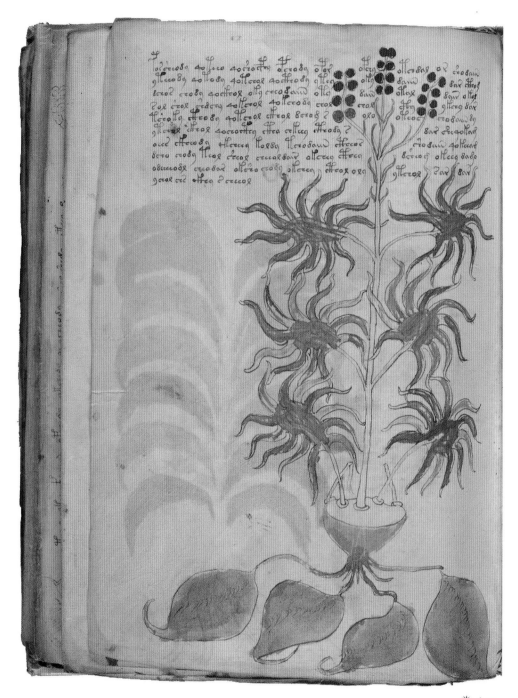

f.94r

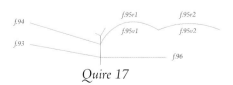

Quire 17

☀ *f.94v*

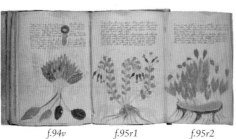

f.94v   *f.95r1*   *f.95r2*

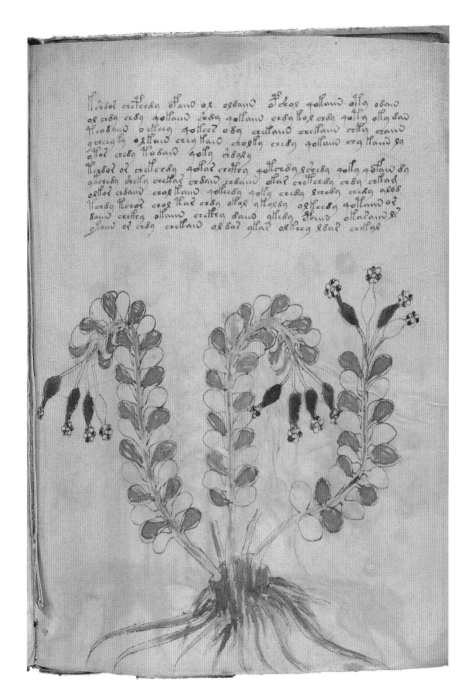

✺ *f.95r1*

Quire 17

❋ *f.95r2*

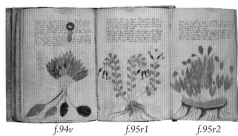

f.94v   *f.95r1*   *f.95r2*   *f.95v2*   *f.95v1*   *f.96r*

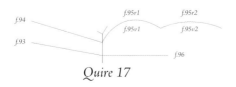
f.95v2

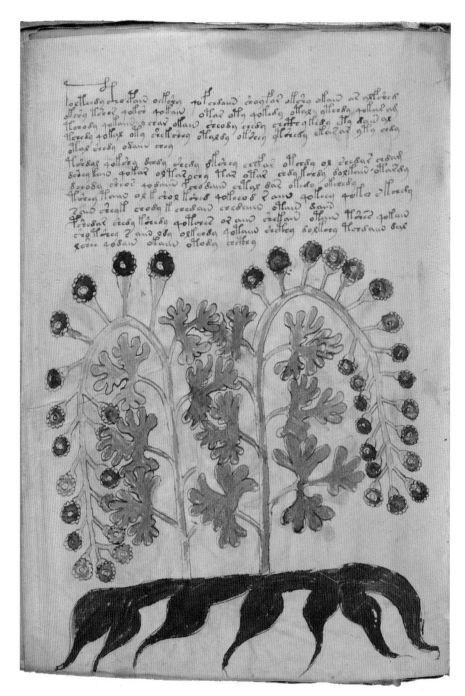

✺ f.95v1

f.95v2   f.95v1   f.96r

✺ *f.96r*

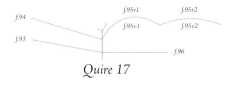

Quire 17

f.96v

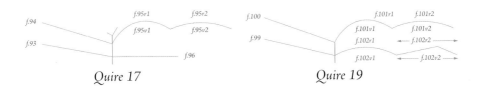

f.100r

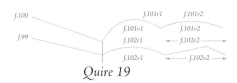

Quire 19

f.100v

f.100v   f.101r1   f.101r2

☀ *f.101r1*

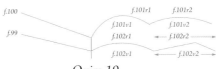

Quire 19

☀ *f.101r2*

f.100v   *f.101r1*   *f.101r2*   *f.101v2*   *f.101v1*   *f.102r1*   *f.102r2*

☀ *f.101v2*

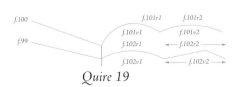

Quire 19

f.101v1

f.101v2   f.101v1   f.102r1   f.102r2

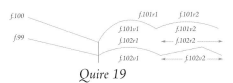

Quire 19

f.102r2

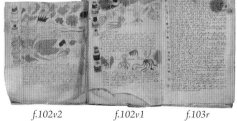

f.101v2   *f.101v1*   *f.102r1*   *f.102r2*   *f.102v2*   *f.102v1*   *f.103r*

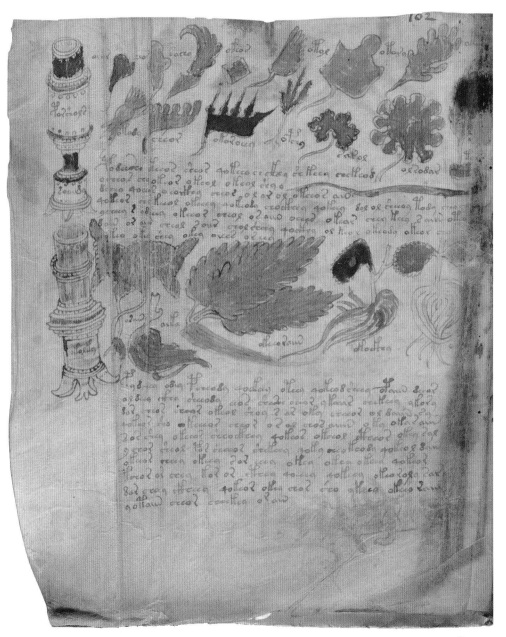

☀ *f.102v2*

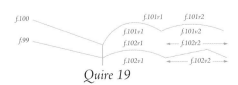

Quire 19

☀ *f.102v1*

f.102v2　　　　*f.102v1*　　　　*f.103r*

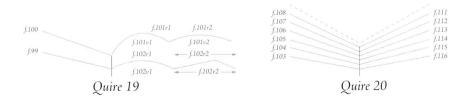

f.103r

Quire 20

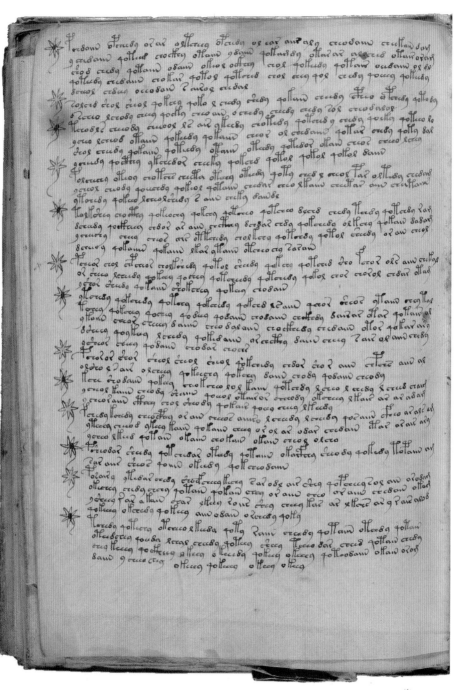

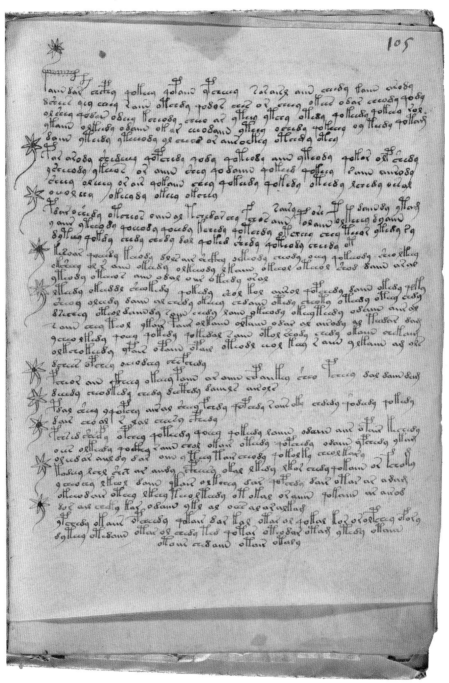

Quire 20

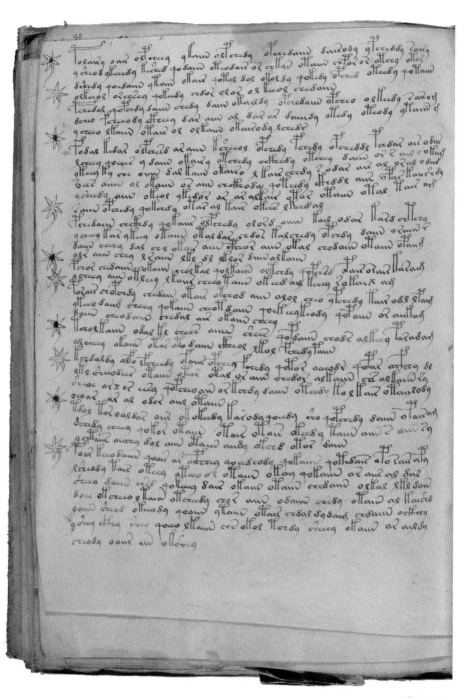

106

f.108 — *f.111*
f.107 — *f.112*
f.106 — *f.113*
f.105 — *f.114*
f.104 — *f.115*
f.103 — *f.116*

Quire 20

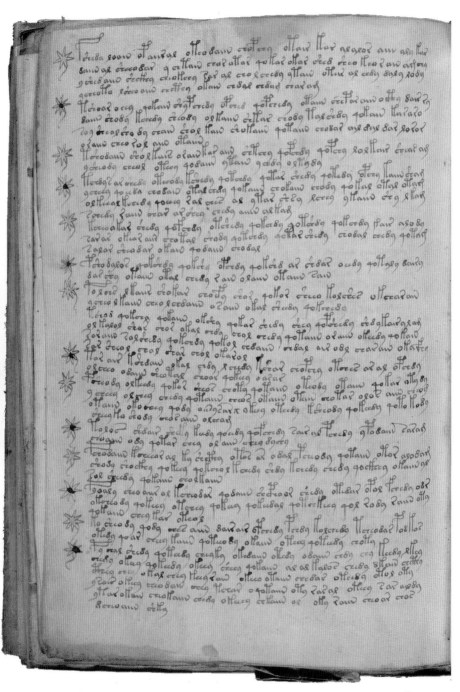

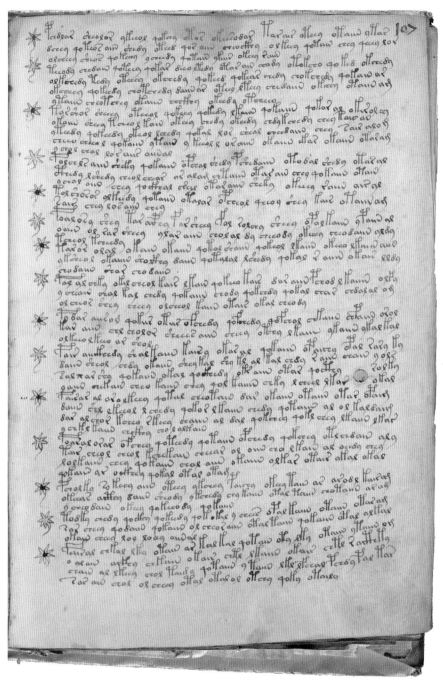

f.107r

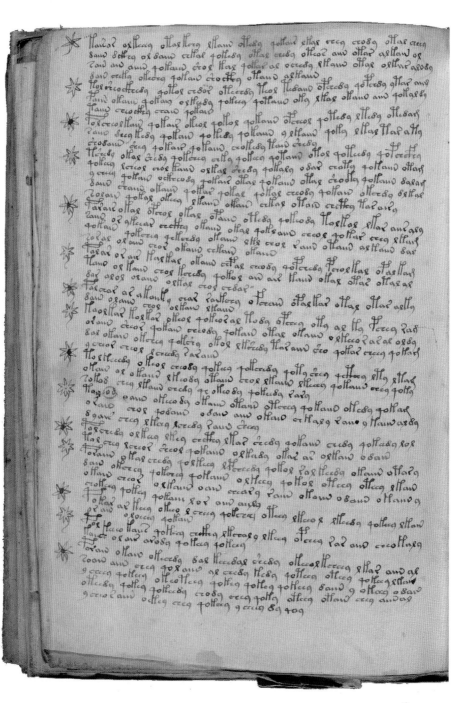

108

f.108r

Quire 20

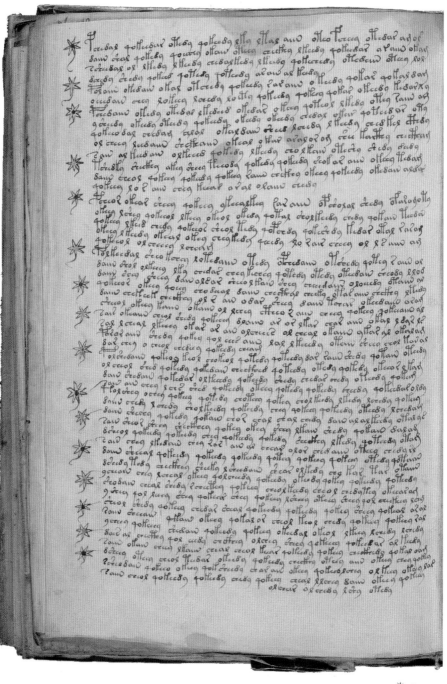

 f.111r

f.108   f.111
f.107   f.112
f.106   f.113
f.105   f.114
f.104   f.115
f.103   f.116

Quire 20

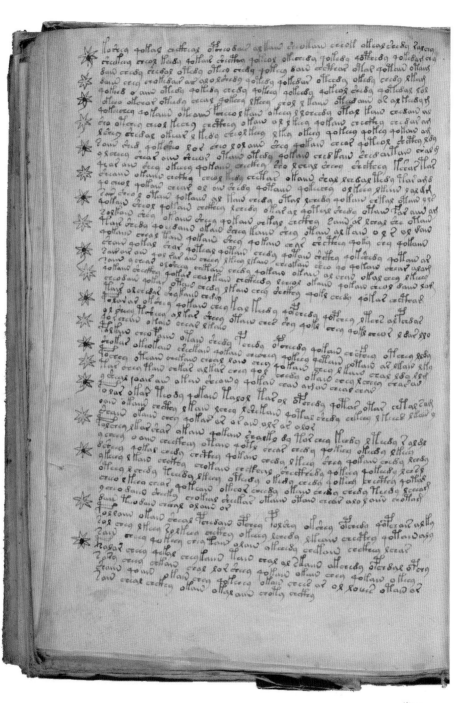

112
13

☀ f.112r

f.108   f.111
f.107   f.112
f.106   f.113
f.105   f.114
f.104   f.115
f.103   f.116

Quire 20

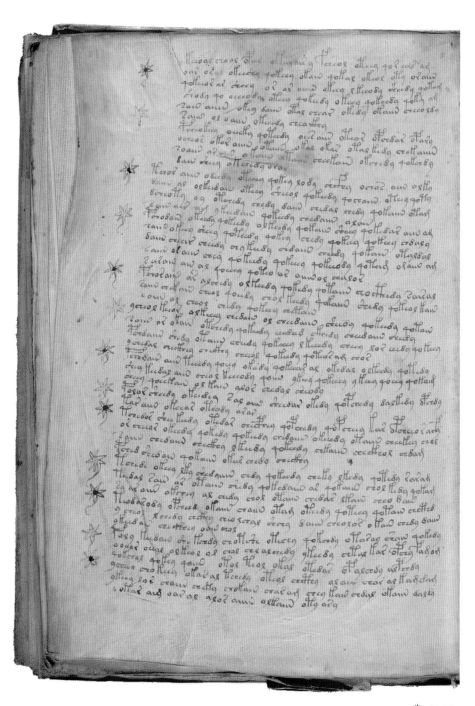

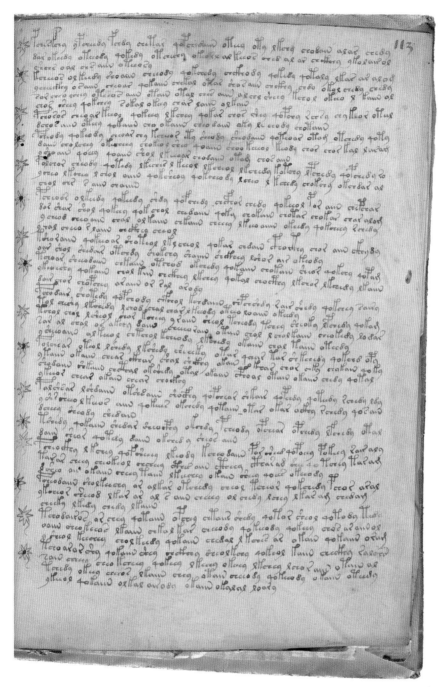

113

f.113r

Quire 20

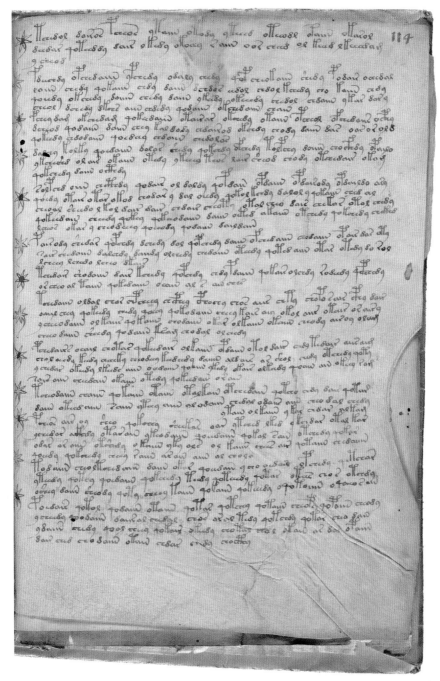

114

Quire 20

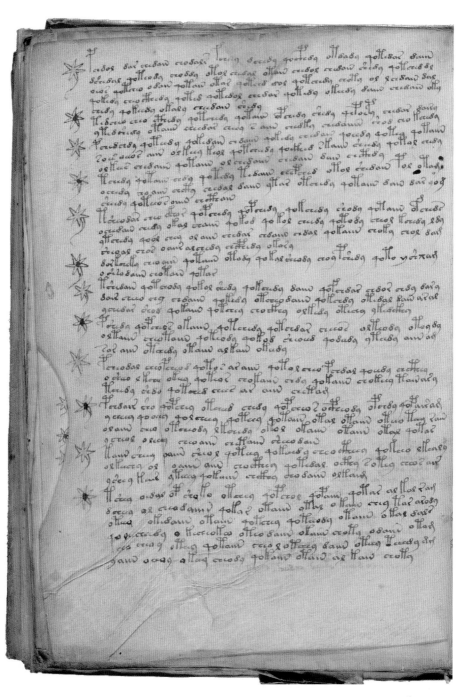

f.114v

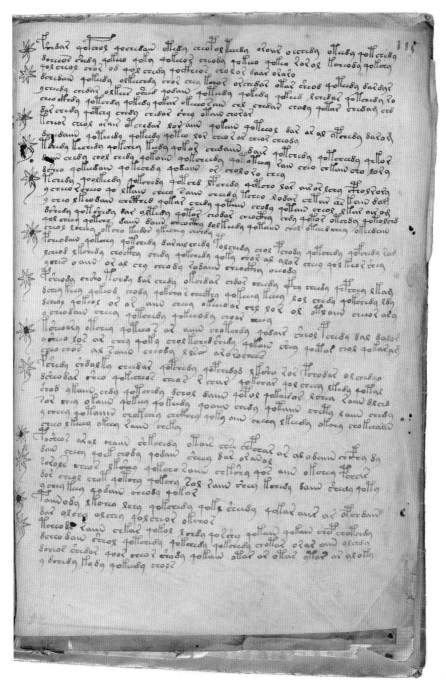

115

f.115r

Quire 20

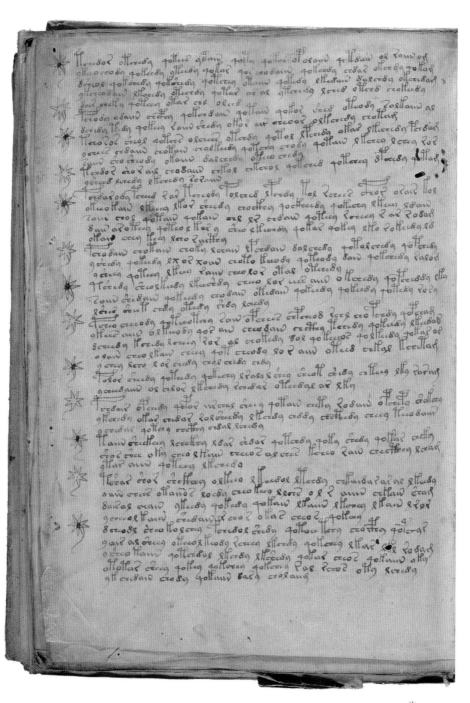

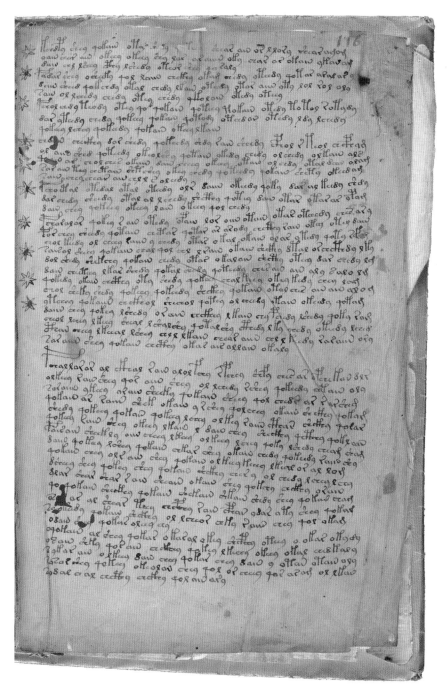

f.116r

Quire 20

❂ *Back flyleaf recto*

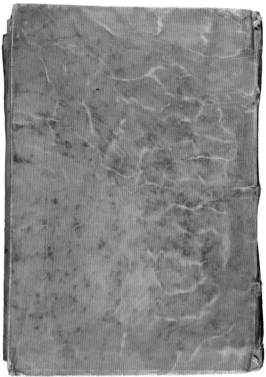

❂ *Back cover*

❂ *Back flyleaf verso*

❂ *Inside back cover*

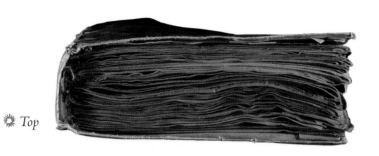

☀ *Top*

☀ *Bottom*

☀ *Spine facing in*

☀ *Spine facing out*

INDEX

WATKINS

Sharing Wisdom Since
1893

The story of Watkins dates back to 1893, when the scholar of esotericism John Watkins founded a bookshop, inspired by the lament of his friend and teacher Madame Blavatsky that there was nowhere in London to buy books on mysticism, occultism or metaphysics. That moment marked the birth of Watkins, soon to become the home of many of the leading lights of spiritual literature, including Carl Jung, Rudolf Steiner, Alice Bailey and Chögyam Trungpa.

Today, the passion at Watkins Publishing for vigorous questioning is still resolute. Our wide-ranging and stimulating list reflects the development of spiritual thinking and new science over the past 120 years. We remain at the cutting edge, committed to publishing books that change lives.

DISCOVER MORE . . .

Read our blog

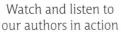

Watch and listen to
our authors in action

Sign up to
our mailing list

JOIN IN THE CONVERSATION

WatkinsPublishing   @watkinswisdom

watkinsbooks   watkinswisdom   watkins-media

Our books celebrate conscious, passionate, wise and happy living.
Be part of the community by visiting

www.watkinspublishing.com